The ever... | ...nising and mem-
orable as any modern military memoir' *Sunday Times*

'Gripping . . . a gifted writer as well as a genuine hero . . . I am
humbled at what these heroes do for us all' *Literary Review*

'The honesty with which Kevin relays his fear, his overwhelming sense that he is going to die, is impressive'
Daily Telegraph

Red One is plain-spoken, hearth-thumping stuff' *The Times*

'[An] absorbing book . . . At the heart of the book is a taut,
exciting account of the events of a single day – February 28,
2006 – when Ivison rushed to the scene of an IED ambush on
a road known as Red One' *Daily Mail*

'One of the most compelling and emotionally honest accounts
of contemporary conflict I've ever read'
Chris Hunter, author of *Extreme Risk*

'But Ivison's bravery in the face of . . . deadly situations is
recounted in colourful detail in *Red One*' *Soldier*

Captain Kevin Ivison was commissioned into the army in 2000, and served in Afghanistan, Bosnia, Kosovo, Northern Ireland and Iraq, where his work as a bomb disposal expert won him the George Medal. Since leaving the army in April 2009 he has established The Counter-IED Consultancy, advising governments, the defence industry and others on all aspects of the counter-IED battle. Visit his website at www.kevinivison.co.uk

RED ONE

*A Bomb Disposal
Expert on the Front Line*

CAPTAIN KEVIN IVISON GM

PHOENIX

A PHOENIX PAPERBACK

First published in Great Britain in 2010
by Weidenfeld & Nicolson
This paperback edition published in 2011
by Phoenix,
an imprint of Orion Books Ltd,
Orion House, 5 Upper St Martin's Lane,
London WC2H 9EA

An Hachette UK company

1 3 5 7 9 10 8 6 4 2

A CIP catalogue record for this book
is available from the British Library.

ISBN 978-0-7538-2830-4

Typeset by Input Data Services Ltd,
Bridgwater, Somerset

Printed and bound in Great Britain by
CPI Mackays, Chatham ME5 8TD

The Orion Publishing Group's policy is to use papers that
are natural, renewable and recyclable products and
made from wood grown in sustainable forests. The logging
and manufacturing processes are expected to conform to
the environmental regulations of the country of origin.

www.orionbooks.co.uk

CONTENTS

ACKNOWLEDGEMENTS

There can seldom have been an author with the good fortune to find such incredible support from his agent and editor; Andrew Lownie and Keith Lowe's belief in me and my story was instant, unswerving and encouraged me greatly as I struggled to articulate a deeply personal account. I must also thank Chris Hunter for his invaluable advice, and Penny Gardiner: her patience and enthusiasm for Red One were phenomenal and her eye for detail second to none.

This story would have ended well before Red One if it were not for Jay and Fitzy. Not only did they keep me alive, but they did it with such humour, professionalism and courage that I was, and still am, in awe of them both. The British Army produces many great soldiers, and I served with two of its best. I also was proud of every second I spent as a member of the Scots Dragoon Guards Battle Group, and was privileged to soldier alongside every Jock and Tom, but I am especially grateful for the advice and support of Eck S, Rhiannon D and Roos A.

I will never be able to repay the friendship, patience and support of my closest friends. They have lived through PTSD with me and I would not be on the path to recovery without their constant help. Chris Y, Ryan C, Mike M, Dave P, Ben S, Lav and the Iron Bridge have listened, sat in silence and laughed with me whenever I needed it. Thank you so much.

At my lowest point, Dr Alicia Deale stepped in and began

to help me put my mind back in order. As long as soldiers see, and do, horrific, terrifying things they will suffer – but with professionals like Alicia to help, they, like I, have a much better chance of getting back to who they once were.

Without the eternal support of my wonderful parents, my journey may have been far shorter. It is their love, support and friendship alone that kept my mind intact; you are both utterly inspirational. And to my wife, who has borne the brunt of PTSD at its worst with a grace, beauty, compassion and love that is beyond comparison, I simply say I love you, and that I cannot wait to spend my whole life with you.

Lastly, to the families of Captain Richard Holmes and Private Lee Ellis who not only provided pictures for this book but whose dignity in the most tragic of circumstance is something few of us could ever aspire to. From what I knew of Richard, and the more I learn of Lee, I am not at all surprised by your strength and amazing courage.

To the people of Wootton Bassett

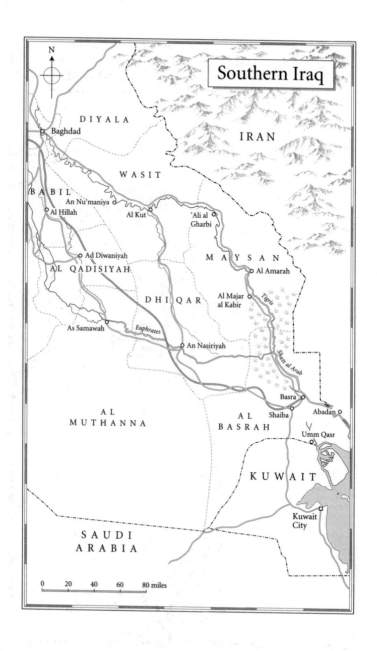

N

Southern Iraq

DIYALA

Baghdad

IRAN

WASIT

BABIL

An Nu'maniya

Al Hillah

Al Kut

'Ali al
Gharbi

MAYSAN

Ad Diwaniyah

AL QADISIYAH

Al Amarah

DHI QAR

Al Majar
al Kabir

Tigris

As Samawah

Euphrates

An Nasiriyah

Shatt al Arab

AL
MUTHANNA

AL
BASRAH

Basra

Shaiba

Abadan

Umm Qasr

KUWAIT

Kuwait
City

SAUDI
ARABIA

0   20   40   60   80 miles

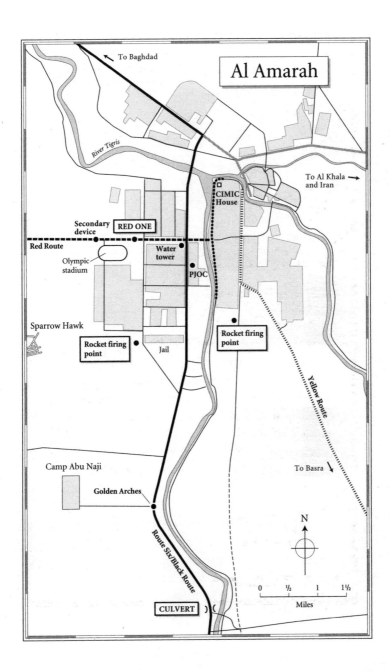

LIST OF ILLUSTRATIONS

from the Queen (by kind permission of British Ceremonial Arts)
30. The George Medal
31. My beautiful wife and me on our wedding day (copyright Ms Melanie Rhys)

Except where otherwise stated, all photographs come from the author's collection. Every effort has been made to trace copyright holders; anyone who has been overlooked is invited to contact the publishers.

PROLOGUE – THE CULVERT

January 2006

I lifted my visor and surveyed the scene, trying to assess the task before me: two bombs, the largest seen in southern Iraq since the coalition had defeated Saddam Hussein's regime over two and a half years ago. My objective was clear: to defuse them. This was the big one: the moment I had dreamt of and trained for since joining the Army seven years earlier.

What I had never imagined all those years ago was the fear. The overwhelming, sickening, paralysing feeling of looking death in the eye. I was now only 20 metres from where I had been told the bombs had been placed, and I felt the familiar high of adrenalin and dread. I had first felt it when training; more so when I defused my first grenade on a military range, and now almost every day, as my team and I took on the Iranian-backed bombers of the Mahdi army. I was facing the most sophisticated bombs in the most dangerous country in the world – and I loved every single moment.

Now, so close to my quarry, it was fight or flight time: the personal, mental battle to shut out every emotion and instinct that screamed at me to walk away and instead, to push myself forward, putting my life on the line once again. So far, fight had won every time.

I was the Ammunition Technical Officer (ATO) – the Army name for a bomb disposal operator – in Al Amarah, the most violent town in Southern Iraq. I had previously deployed to the roughest parts of Northern Ireland, throughout the Balkans and even to Afghanistan, but Al Amarah was something else entirely. This was bandit country, a 'Wild West' frontier town on the border with Iran where so much British blood had already been spilt since Saddam's regime had been destroyed in 2003.

Seven successive British Battle Groups had garrisoned this town since the ground war ended and in that time had won every fight, every contact and every engagement except for the most important one of all – the battle for hearts and minds. Even now, three years after British troops first arrived in Al Amarah, with so many lives cut short and with millions of pounds poured into reconstruction projects, the locals still detested our presence and frequently let us know it, raining high explosive rockets on to our camp at night and blowing up patrols during the day. It was my job to protect the Scots Dragoon Guards Battle Group from both. So far we had lost no one to either. I wasn't about to let that change today.

I stood on Route 6, the main artery between Basra, Al Amarah and Baghdad and looked around. The terrain was flat and dusty, punctuated only by the huge tarmac road – beneath which lay my prey – and the occasional small brick factory from which long plumes of smoke poured incessantly. The smell of burning clay hung everywhere in Al Amarah giving the town a distinctive smoggy atmosphere and yellow-tinged air. The smell was inescapable except in dense urban areas when it was overpowered by the stench of sewage that flowed non-stop in neglected broken pipes beside and underneath the road.

To my left and right, Challenger 2 tanks and Warrior armoured fighting vehicles took up positions in the cordon that was responsible for protecting me from the snipers lurking in the small villages nearby and, more importantly, protecting the locals from the explosive power of what I was sure would be the most devastating IEDs (Improvised Explosive Device) we had ever seen. Tank commanders armed with binoculars appeared from turrets and, upon spotting potential snipers disappeared back inside to spin the turret and look through infrared sights before reappearing and beginning the process again. Looking into the barrel of a 120mm cannon with its high explosive payload and hearing the grunt of 72 tonnes of armour swivelling toward them had so far persuaded all would-be assassins that today was not the best day to fight.

The tanks constantly sought better vantage points and prowled the flat areas at the sides of the road for the ideal spot from which to see as much of the area as possible and unleash their awesome firepower if necessary. This was excellent tank country: flat, featureless terrain where no one could escape the infrared sights, high explosive rounds, 7.62mm machine gun or depleted uranium darts which would spew out from this fighting machine when required.

As the rear door of each Warrior sprang open, seven infantrymen sprinted out, zigzagging toward cover behind rocks and in natural dips in the ground. Experienced eyes peered through the thermal imaging sight of the Warrior and the SUSAT sights of the men's SA80s and Minimi machine guns. Inside each armoured vehicle a foot hovered over the trigger pedal which could loose off 30mm high explosive rounds at any assailant within 1.5 kilometres of us, destroying all but the hardest targets.

Overhead a Lynx helicopter circled, the gunner sitting in the left-hand door eyeing likely enemy positions, always ready to swoop and let loose a storm of 7.62mm. Higher still, an American F-18 Hornet kept watch over us all, its phenomenal arsenal invisible to both us and our enemies on the ground, but ready to hurtle down and evaporate anyone who had chosen today to fight. If anyone was suicidal enough to take us on, they would feel the effect of my 'Love from above' before the echo of their own shot had faded.

This awesome military machine had one role today: to help me defuse these bombs and let the people of Al Amarah carry on with their daily lives.

For a few hours I was definitely the biggest kid in the playground.

Only a short while ago, an Iraqi Police agent had told us that two bombs had been placed in a culvert underneath the road. The culverts acted as drainage pipes, were less than a metre high, ran the full width of the road and, along Route 6, were spaced every 200 metres. Over time, many of them had gradually filled with sewage, mud, debris and, in Al Amarah, IEDs too.

The agent had described seeing 'dragon bombs' – a local term for shaped charges. These devices were capable of punching through the thickest armour and even a tank crew would be left with no chance of survival. Anyone patrolling along the road would see neither the culvert nor its deadly contents before the road erupted beneath him.

The Passive InfraRed (PIR) detector would sense the heat of an armoured vehicle and transmit an electronic signal to the detonator, which sends a supersonic shockwave at over 8,000 metres per second throughout the C4 explosive that comprises the bulk of the bomb. The blast alone would tear up the road and hurl a 30-tonne Warrior tens of metres on to its roof, crushing the occupants. Worse than that, the detonation wave would also strike a copper cone inserted into one end of the explosive which would collapse in on itself and create an unstoppable jet of molten metal, burning through the armour and cooking anyone inside. It wasn't called the dragon for nothing.

I would be vaporized if I was within 100 metres of one of them when it exploded.

It wasn't just the bombs; I had other problems to deal with. A traffic jam had been caused by the cordon blocking the road and even here, in no man's land, 100 metres away from the nearest car, I could see that the locals were getting seriously pissed off. Men who had been initially good tempered were now leaving their cars and approaching the infantry, demanding to be let through. They pointed furiously at young children crying in the back of cars and at fresh produce in trucks destined for markets in Al Amarah. Interpreters struggled to relay the reason for the delay; if anyone drove along the road it could trigger an explosion, killing the driver and anyone else within 100 metres. Angry men returned to their cars, fists clenched and arms waving, and encouraged others to do the same. Tempers were red hot.

My radio burst into life.

'This needs to be quick, ATO.' Even the unflappable infantry commander Sergeant Spire sounded nervous, his deep Glaswegian accent almost drowned out by the noise from the crowd. 'Them fuckers are getting angry.'

It was getting worse. At the southern cordon another group of Iraqi men were remonstrating with the troops. One was being held back by another as he tried to run towards a Warrior, clutching his shoe in his right hand, the ultimate Iraqi insult. More cars joined the queue every minute and pressure was building.

The area was perfect for snipers and terrorist bombers and I was standing in the middle of the only road in and out of this location, making my movements easy to predict. For all I knew, there may have been secondary devices littering my route to the culvert, unseen so far, waiting tirelessly for my arrival. I could have been in the middle of a cross hair from the moment

I stepped out of my Bucher Duro EOD van. The sniper would only get one shot before the hail of metal and high explosive wiped him from the face of the earth, but that would be enough. Only one week earlier, Corporal Alan Douglas was taking down a communications mast on top the police station in town and never even heard the shot that killed him.

Tasks outside camp were undoubtedly exhilarating – and what we had all joined the Army for – but each of us was aware that we were very much on borrowed time, just one wrong move, one squeeze of the trigger away from death. A lot of young British lives had ended in this town over the last few years and there were plenty of people capable of causing much more bloodshed if they wished.

I walked slowly forwards again, searching for anything that looked out of place, something the wrong shade of sandy yellow, something too new, too expensive to belong here, something that wasn't there yesterday, something that just looked ... wrong. A soldier's life depended a lot on nothing more than intuition, the indefinable feeling that let you know when the trouble was going to start. After nearly three months of hunting bombs on the streets of Al Amarah, my intuition was very good; but then, so was my enemy.

This task was going to have to be carried out with my hands: no robots, no weapons, no laser beams, no James Bond gadgets, just me and a pair of pliers. The MOD spent millions of pounds on sophisticated robots that were ideal in London or Manchester but useless in Iraq. My robot often simply broke down in the Iraqi heat and had no chance of getting down the steep muddy slope to the culvert. All that money spent on sophisticated robots, and I was facing two of the biggest bombs ever seen with nothing more than a pair of pliers.

An ATO would usually wear a heavy armoured suit to guard against blast and fragmentation, but today there was no chance of that: the culverts were too small, so there was no way I could get out in a hurry if something went wrong. Instead, I wore my standard issue body armour and helmet. It would offer no protection from bombs of this size, but it might mean that a bit more of me would remain intact if they did detonate; if I was lucky I might not completely evaporate.

I was taking too long. The fear was building inside and the excitement had long since drained away. The mental battle was always tougher than the physical one.

Fight or flight.

My heart thumped until I thought I could hear it pounding against the ceramic plates covering my chest inside my armour, sweat streamed down my face and obscured my vision, my brain ran at 1,000 miles per hour and my legs felt like lead.

I moved forward.

Seeing action, the crowd became even more excited and stood on car bonnets, shouting, screaming and pointing at the lone soldier edging towards the culvert. Iraqis were no strangers to violence and had seen many ATOs undertake similar tasks. This was my first tour in Iraq; the Iraqis were far more aware than I was of Al Amarah's insurgents and knew just how vulnerable I was. I just hoped the crowd would stay excited and not become bored – I would be in real trouble if they tried to get through the cordon. The reassuring weight of my SA80 rifle and the Browning pistol strapped to my leg gave me some comfort, but I'd have had it if they surged.

I moved forward slowly, stopping after every step, observing, desperate to see anything which would give me a clue as to how these bombs were triggered. I knew there would be a PIR switch hidden somewhere, but there could also be a pressure switch, a tripwire or even a radio control pack. I had some control over the first two, but was absolutely reliant on Fitzy, my Electronic Countermeasures (ECM) Operator or 'Bleep' to protect me from radio-controlled bombs. So much of being a bomb disposal operator was about placing your life in others hands. I thanked God, Allah, whoever was listening that I had the team I did.

'South cordon is taking some shit now – these guys are fucking pissed off.' Over the radio I could hear the crowd shouting and screaming whenever Sergeant Spire spoke. If I rushed I would die. I just had to hope that the cordon could hold out.

Another step forward. I remembered what the boss of the Weapons Intelligence Section (WIS) had told me on the secure line minutes before I left camp.

'We must recover these things intact – we need to know exactly how they were built.' WIS was a secretive branch of the Divisional intelligence cell whose sole job was to work out who was planting IEDs, what they were capable of and how to defeat them. Luckily for me, WIS was made up of former ATOs, who fully understood the dangers involved in recovering an IED, although most of them hadn't defused a bomb in years. I could have blown these things up and been back in camp for tea and medals an hour ago, but they were right: if I recovered them, lives could be saved in the future.

Life as a bomb disposal operator was incredibly surreal: it was a running joke at home that I could barely wire a plug, and yet here I was at the business end of one of the most important bomb disposal tasks of the conflict so far. If I didn't recover these bombs intact we would never know how to defeat them. This task was about many more lives than my own.

Walk, stop, observe; walk, stop, observe; breathe. By the time I was within 10 metres of the culvert I was exhausted, my combats soaked with sweat. It was not so much the physical exertion of carrying my equipment, but the mental fatigue of intense concentration and the constant fear that someone, somewhere may choose to press a button, attach a battery or connect the wire at any moment, triggering the device and turning me into red mist.

I stopped 5 metres short of the culvert, lay on my front and took in every detail before me. I was not looking for big battery packs, large burning fuses or sticks of dynamite strapped together; my enemy was far too capable to leave obvious signs. Like an animal tracker, I looked for the tiniest detail that might give an indication of what lay ahead: footprints, discarded cigarettes, pieces of paper and drag marks were all signals that something had happened here recently. In training I was also told to be suspicious if I encountered 'the absence of the normal, the presence of the abnormal'. If this area looked as if it had been tidied up, that would be just as suspect as seeing footprints leading into the culvert.

In addition to the unintentional signs of activity I also looked for any deliberate signs of danger. IEDs, like minefields, are often marked, to make life easier for the insurgent. If my enemy was 300 metres away waiting for me to crawl up to the bomb before initiating it, he would need to know two things: where I was and where the bomb was.

This is not as easy as it sounds.

The enemy tactic of camouflaging IEDs often made it extremely difficult for them to see their own devices. No doubt the insurgent could see me easily – after all, there was only one man crawling slowly along this 200-metre stretch of road – so he might choose to mark the location of the bomb with something obvious. He could leave a small pile of stones at the side of the road, place his bomb near a lamp-post with a flag hanging at its top or even hide his bomb in some obvious street furniture. From that point, targeting was very simple: wait until I, a tank or any other patrol got close to the marker and it would all be over. The enemy would have pressed the button and disappeared from view before the smoke had drifted from the crater.

I could see nothing. Nothing unusual at all. It would be very difficult to move two heavy shaped charges without leaving any sign whatsoever. My heart sank. Maybe this was a 'false' or a 'hoax' – an operation that required huge amounts of effort and put many people in harm's way, outside the protection of the camp, for nothing. Tasks like this were common, chipped away at morale and depleted my team's limited reserves of courage, adrenaline and patience for no real gain.

I should have known better than to trust the Iraqi Police; they were corrupt, notoriously unreliable and had been accomplices in more than one British fatality.

It mattered little. There was no way I could declare the site safe until I had fully examined every part of it. My drills and skills had to remain immaculate regardless of the likelihood of finding a device. If I got sloppy and word got back to the insurgents, they would exploit it and I would be history. Worse still, they could target my replacement.

Only a short, steep, filthy slope lay between me and the dry stream bed which marked the opening of the culvert. Inch by inch I moved forward, every discarded Coke can, plastic bag and small mound checked by sight, metal detector and hand before edging a fraction forward. Better ATOs than I had lost limbs and even their lives due to tiny errors of judgement or simple misfortune, so I was absolutely meticulous, with no part of my body straying from my cleared 'safe lane'. If nothing else, a 'false' task like this was good practice for the real thing.

My PRR buzzed with the usual cordon chatter – although they were stationary there was a constant need for updates.

'Red car approaching, slowing, two male occupants.'

'Roger.'

'Car stopped – no threat.'

While I was so exposed, the chatter was reassuring. I had only to concentrate on my task; the really tough job of controlling the crowd was left to the cordon troops.

I crept forward a little more. The stream bed that ran through the culvert was strewn with litter, sewage, rotting weeds and the ubiquitous Coke bottles. Now, at the bottom of the slope, I could peer right into the culvert. It was dark, cold and even narrower than I had imagined. Faint shadows only a few metres into the darkness caught my eye, probably more rubbish that had been washed underneath. I crawled in and felt my chest tighten and my pulse rise with a wave of claustrophobia. Only moments after I disappeared inside the culvert my PRR erupted with noise.

'STOP OR I'LL FUCKING SHOOT!', someone screamed.

'ATO, GET THE FUCK OUT OF THERE!' Sergeant Spire's voice.

'STOP STOP STOP, FUCKING STOP!' another voice echoed around the culvert.

Shit – someone was near me.

The sound of a weapon being cocked was both unmistakable and terrifying as I was briefly trapped underground. My claustrophobia was quickly forgotten as I threw myself out of the culvert, grabbed my SA80 rifle and sprinted up the bank to the road, through the area that I had just cleared.

It was mayhem.

A red car had breached the perimeter to my left. Racing towards it from my right was the Royal Engineers Search Advisor (RESA), Sergeant Jones, with his rifle raised. I was standing in the middle of the road with a suicidal driver speeding towards me, and every chance of 5.56mm rounds zipping in the opposite direction. Above me the Lynx was dropping like a stone to turn this car into a colander if it went any further. At the same time, half a dozen Perkins engines roared into life as the Challengers and Warriors spun towards the road.

The car slowed and the whole world fell deadly silent.

It wasn't just me who faced fight or flight today; inside the car a middle-aged Iraqi stayed perfectly still for a moment, his eyes fixed on the road ahead, trying to ignore the volume of armaments trained at his head.

Fight or flight.

'Get out of the car!' Sergeant Jones had run from the cordon and was now only 20 metres to my right, his rifle pinned to his shoulder, the red laser attached to his barrel darting up and down with his laboured breathing, but never leaving the face of the driver.

Flight.

Our new friend held his hands in the air and slumped into his seat, cursing loudly. It was impatience, not malice, that had caused him to breach the cordon, but the threat of suicide bombers in Al Amarah was high. He very nearly lost his life because of it.

Our pulses were raised and the crowd knew it; they had seen our reaction to a single vehicle and knew there would be no second chances.

With tensions high it was now more important than ever to get this over with quickly. Back at the culvert I began my search again; it was about 10 metres long and I had searched only 2 metres of it. I would do the rest quickly, out of sight of the enemy, and get out of there.

Drag marks.

I froze; the marks were deep and led to the shadows I had seen earlier. Was this it? I continued to search carefully, centimetre by centimetre, using both hands. Progress was agonizingly slow as I inched forward, my small mouth-torch allowing only 30 centimetres of visibility.

I knew the enemy well and tried to imagine how they would have planned this attack. It would be so easy to put a booby trap down here and kill me. They would know that my robot could never get in here and that I would have no option but to clear the area myself. It would be easy to hide a small pressure-activated IED inside the culvert. One false move, one lapse in concentration . . . I didn't even want to think about it.

Amidst the filth of the culvert was old discarded wire and the remnants of a broken TV that had been dumped at the other end of the culvert and over the years had been eroded by the stream. Old rusted circuit boards and wire had broken off, and over time had embedded themselves in the mud. The enemy had chosen a site where everything looked like a bomb. They were so good.

Every item could be booby-trapped, and I struggled to maintain my discipline as I searched around each object before throwing it behind me and carrying on. Time was short and I was getting frustrated. My PRR had long gone silent due to the mass of concrete above me and I had no idea what state the crowd were in.

By now I must only be half a metre away from where I had seen the shadows earlier. Placing my metal detector down in front of me I searched for pressure pads and loose trip wires with my fingertips. This was bomb disposal at its most basic.

Moments later I retreated toward the entrance to the culvert, slumped against the bank and held my PRR. It had been a long day. I reached for the small green press-to-talk switch and a familiar electronic beep let me know I was transmitting.

'Bingo! Got them.'

1. BUILD UP

I was born in Shrewsbury in May 1981 and lived in military quarters and barracks in Shropshire and York before the whole family – Mum, Dad, my sister Sarah and I – left the UK in 1984 for five years on the front line of the Cold War in Germany.

Dad was an infantryman – a Warrant Officer Class Two by the time his 25-year-career ended – and I spent much of my remarkably happy childhood clambering over armoured vehicles, firing rifles and running over assault courses. I loved it. The Army felt natural, like family. It was home.

Nevertheless, the streets of Al Amarah, fighting in Iraq or becoming a bomb disposal operator were beyond my imagination as aged 8, I looked out of the window of my school in Germany and saw soldiers with heavy packs sprinting past, their faces covered with camouflage paint and creased with pain.

Every couple of months a long snake of 432 Armoured Personnel Carriers (APC) would rumble past, hundreds of tonnes of armour shaking the classroom, rattling the windows and causing my heart to race. From the commander's hatch of the lead vehicle a man with a face covered in mud would appear, always wearing the same green helmet covered with twigs and leaves, his goggles encrusted with dirt, his skin tainted by worn-in camouflage paint and eyes that looked as if he hadn't slept for days. As I waved excitedly, Dad would throw up a mock salute in return, his unmistakable smile breaking through the layers of paint, filth and tiredness. He was returning from exercise and I wouldn't have seen him for at least three weeks.

I listened intently when Dad returned from exercise to our tiny flat in Paderborn to tell me that he had once again beaten the Russians, that he had personally accounted for the destruction of a least a dozen enemy armoured personnel carriers with his precision mortar fire, and that we could sleep safely once again. The 50,000-man British Army of the Rhine (BAOR), Dad told me, was all that stood between the massive Soviet forces – constantly poised, ready to strike – and Britain.

The first time I ever saw a Russian in real life, he was pointing a rifle at my mother. We had travelled to Berlin in 1988 to peek behind the Iron Curtain when my mum had opened the car door at Checkpoint Charlie in order to relieve the stifling summer heat. That sound, the metallic clatter of rifle working parts slamming into position, seemed to last a lifetime as the guard screamed at her to get back in the car. Even my Dad, in full dress uniform, could do nothing as more rifles swung towards us. I was 7 years old but already had a very strong sense of right and wrong; pointing a rifle at a woman trying to cool her children down was wrong, and the frustration of my inaction burned inside me.

Life as a child in BAOR was to live a life under threat. The Cold War simmered constantly without ever boiling over, but the conflict with the Provisional IRA exploded with regular, predictable certainty. Even in Germany, hundreds of miles from the streets of Belfast, the Provisionals haunted us with their bullets and bombs: I knew how to check for booby-traps under a car ten years before I learned to drive one.

Some of my starkest memories are of terrorist acts. For a 7-year-old, the hours locked indoors as bomb disposal teams combed the area outside our flat after another warning were thrilling; watching my father stare at the television as the news relayed yet more stories of soldiers being shot, blown up or butchered, was not.

Looking back, I was always going to join the Army; it just took me a few years to realize it.

My childhood had been militarily nomadic, moving from home to home as my father's Army career led us from my birthplace of Shropshire to York, Germany and finally Lancashire. At secondary school I briefly flirted with the idea of becoming an illustrator, an actor, a lawyer or an engineering apprentice, but these romances were all short-lived. I had no idea what I wanted to do, but I knew that most normal jobs just didn't fit the bill. Something was missing; I needed to be passionate about my chosen career.

My father left the Army in 1994. For the next two years I barely thought of soldiers, tanks or guns, until I attended an Army awareness day organized by my school. Within minutes of arriving at Fulwood Barracks in Preston, however, I was hooked, the sight of armoured vehicles and soldiers, the smells of camouflage netting and green tents and the sounds of bullets cracking through the air taking me straight back to my child-hood. I had grown up with the Army and hadn't even realized how much I had missed it.

'Mum, I'm joining the Army!' My 15-year-old face was alight with excitement. My mother, having only recently seen her husband retire, and terrified of losing her son to the military, wept the tears of someone who had waited for this inevitable but nonetheless painful day to arrive.

She sniffed as she mopped at her tears:

'Me and your dad will support you whatever you decide to do, but for God's sake at least join as an officer.' She carefully explained that officers started at a higher rank, had the potential to earn more money and appeared to have an easier, more glamorous life.

I was sold.

That night, the stack of war memoirs that my dad had collected over the years was piled up by the side of my bed and I began to read. My thirst for information was unquenchable; personal accounts of the Falklands War, the Gulf War and the Troubles in Northern Ireland left me spellbound into the early hours.

The Falklands War set my imagination on fire; this was the rawest of wars, attrition by two infantry-based armies meeting at close quarters, often within bayonet range, victory achieved only by the brutal application of force and extreme violence of a kind I could barely comprehend. It was the rawness of the combat that kept me turning the pages, man versus man, my skill against your skill, my strength against your strength. This wasn't a war of high technology; battles were not won by Tomahawk Cruise missiles, stealth fighters or pilotless drones; this was filthy, exhausting, bloody combat of the most basic kind, the kind that had barely changed since the evolution of mankind.

Just as fascinating as the battles were accounts of the long periods of inaction, of waiting. Many writers described the incessant shelling from Argentinean mortars and artillery on dug-in British troops, and its effect on their minds. Initially these attacks caused terror and confusion, then the soldiers seemed to cope by developing an almost apathetic attitude, a complacency towards the menace posed by these barrages. But even an instrument as sophisticated as the human mind could only take so much, the mortars gradually chipping away at the courage of those on the receiving end. Men became irritable, angry, sometimes very quiet and occasionally cracked under the increasing pressure of endless fear they named shell shock.

I wondered how it was possible to deal with such sustained onslaught? If some of the finest fighting troops in the world could become ineffective after this kind of mental torture how on earth would I cope?

The first Gulf War in 1991 already seemed more distant, less personal and more clinical in its application of force. This was a war of science, of technology and of the 'Smart Bomb'. Half a decade earlier I had watched in awe as the news showed high explosive missiles entering pre-selected windows in target buildings, after skimming along the ocean for hundreds of miles. Was this the new kind of combat? Had soldiers been removed from war, replaced by circuit boards and infrared seeker heads, relegated to the occasional skirmish to mop up a woefully under-equipped enemy who was quicker to surrender than fight?

The images of Apache gunships, F-117 Nighthawk stealth bombers and Patriot missiles were seen through the grainy, green-tinged night vision cameras that characterized the war. This was a very different kind of combat, but it was no less enthralling.

Northern Ireland was different altogether and held the most fascination for me. My father had served in Northern Ireland for a large portion of his career and had often told me of his experiences. The near misses, such as the time he tripped over a can of paint, only to see the wall behind him sprayed with a long line of bullets; the blowing up by terrorist bombs of members of his battalion and the constant threat posed by the Provisional IRA; the never opening a car door without first searching underneath it for bombs.

The Troubles was a war on my doorstep, and due to my Irish Catholic roots, one that felt much more personal than the others. I was sickened by the brutality of the terrorists' attacks – such as at Warrenpoint, when eighteen British soldiers were killed by an IRA bomb, and the Remembrance Day killings in Enniskillen – and I was also amazed by the ineptitude of the British strategy to win peace. Internment seemed to be the most effective way that I could think of to energize the extremist Republican population.

As I read of the Shankhill Butchers who abducted, tortured and slashed their way through at least thirty lives, and the harrowing killing of the two Royal Signals Corporals who mistakenly drove into a Republican funeral, I tried to understand the hatred that defined this conflict.

The Troubles were about more than just a border, religion or which side of the peace wall a family lived. There seemed to be too much hatred, too much history and too much blood spilt to ever imagine a peaceful outcome. This was my first foray into the world of lies, deceit, bullets and bombs that is terrorism, and the aim of winning over a population rather than just beating them into submission. This kind of conflict seemed to be the most intellectually taxing of all. No one would carpet bomb Belfast, no smart bombs would be dropped through Londonderry windows, but still the battle had to be won.

From my reading I saw that there appeared to be two kinds of courage: the fiery courage that was seen during the attacks on Tumbledown and Mount Longdon, and the colder, calmer courage required to survive mentally through mortar bombardments and long patrols through the rolling, deadly, fields of South Armagh. Courage was an indefinable, immeasurable quality that was highly prized but barely understood. What on earth made a man better in combat than the person next to him? How did people perform incredible acts of bravery when the odds seemed hopelessly stacked against them?

How would I cope?

Even in my mid teens I knew there would be only one way to answer that question. The only thing of which I was absolutely certain was that I had found my calling – my passion.

My route to Sandhurst took in a two-year spell at Welbeck College, an Army-funded boarding school for those intending to pursue a career as an army officer. It fed my appetite for long sports afternoons, leadership training and interaction with the military units that visited frequently. My love for all things military, sporting and adventurous surpassed my love of all things academic by some distance, and I barely scraped through each term, never rising above the bottom quarter. Thankfully my grades were just good enough for entry to Sandhurst and I was awarded a place starting in January 2000.

Before Sandhurst, and seeing an opportunity for a spot of adventure, I arranged a three-month attachment to my father's old battalion, the 1st Battalion, The Queen's Lancashire Regiment (1 QLR) who were based in Omagh, Northern Ireland. Only a year had passed since a huge car bomb exploded in the centre of the town, killing twenty-nine people, and reminders of that day were everywhere. The shock of it still reverberated through 1 QLR and the locals who had suffered and were still suffering as a result of it.

Within a month of arriving and immersing myself in the rhythm of life in an infantry battalion I had noticed that one building in camp was off limits to all but a select few. Sirens frequently blared across the barracks as the bomb disposal team sped from this building in their Tactica armoured vehicles. Myths surrounded the nerve, courage and capabilities of these men, known universally as 'Felix' or ATO. They lived alone, separate from the remainder of 1 QLR, emerging from their compound only for emergencies and seemingly accorded God-like status from the battalion and wider Army.

There were only six ATOs in Northern Ireland, and no one

else was deemed capable of taking on the Provisional IRA's best bomb-makers. The ATO's word was law. It mattered little if he was a sergeant and the infantry incident commander was a warrant officer, captain or colonel – during bomb disposal operations he outranked them all.

I frequently found reasons to walk past the secluded ATO compound. It was adorned on the outside with items I knew to be improvised mortars such as the infamous Provisional IRA Barrack Buster with its devastating high explosive payload. Through the wire fence it was possible to see strange-looking robots being contorted into obscure shapes by operators clutching remote controls. Others ferried thick green suits from the back of the Tactica to the offices – suits I had seen on television being worn by bomb disposal men. I was seeing a very different side of the Army to life in an infantry battalion. There was no shouting or parades; just a very close-knit team doing what they had to do.

I couldn't leave Omagh without finding out as much as I could about these men, so I found myself volunteering to join another group of potential officers as they visited the many different areas of the battalion. I sat still, barely moving, as the ATO described the threat from IEDs in Northern Ireland, including a Barrack Buster which had been fired at Bessbrook Mill in South Armagh. Entranced, I whistled involuntarily as he showed pictures of the aftermath of the Omagh bomb and recent car bombs in Belfast.

The ATO explained that he not only led the team but was also responsible for walking down the road and defusing the bombs – 'The Longest Walk'. There was no delegation; no one else in the team could fulfil that role, only the main man. The buck started and stopped with him.

This was the stuff of Action Man or James Bond; one man responsible for dismantling, with his own hands, car bombs, mortars, anything the terrorists could dream up, pitting his wits against those of the terrorist. This was not a war of attrition but one of cunning deceit; often the various factions of the IRA would plant multiple IEDs or fake devices specifically to lure an ATO to the area before taking him on with another bomb. Whenever the Provisional IRA killed a bomb disposal man it was not only a political victory – until he was replaced they would have the opportunity to cause mayhem.

This intellectual combat had evolved to a point where devices often concealed other, smaller, booby traps inside them, or where the bodies of people who had been murdered were used to disguise bombs concealed nearby. This was chess, with the highest possible stakes.

ATOs typically served for six months in Northern Ireland and returned home for a year or so before being called back. Although only the most able and experienced operators deployed to the Province, the men they were facing, the bombers, were born and bred into terrorism and had even greater experience. A grudging respect had developed between these two bitter enemies as each tried to outmanoeuvre the other.

Although undoubtedly brave, ATOs did not run forward with bags of grenades or bayonet the enemy, full of adrenalin, or in last-ditch efforts to save their own lives. This was the same cold courage that allowed men to operate under heavy fire in the Falklands. Each step, each action, was planned meticulously, in full awareness of its potential consequences. Many ATOs had died performing this work and many more had been maimed. The lucky few had been recognized for their work, with two George Crosses, twenty-nine George Medals and nearly three hundred other awards for bravery being awarded since the Troubles began.

The ATO saw my wide eyes and ended on a flourish:

'So my job . . .' he paused for effect, 'is to get in there before these things explode, and make them safe.'

I could barely take it in; the responsibility, complexity and challenge of counter-terrorist bomb disposal seemed unimaginable. And yet I knew this was everything I had ever wanted. I had made up my mind: I would move heaven and earth to become an ATO.

The steep steps which led to Old College at the Royal Military Academy Sandhurst loomed in the distance as my parents dropped me off at the Academy where I would spend the next year of my life. Aged 18, I was the youngest Officer Cadet in my intake by some margin; everyone else seeming so old, so well rounded and so much more relaxed about the experience. To me, it was everything.

In my platoon some had already had other successful careers: one had left a lucrative job in the City to pursue a life of adventure, most had come straight from university and only a few of us did not have degrees. I was a boy in a man's world.

Thirty per cent of the formidable Sandhurst training was delivered outside, on exercise, where we slept under thin plastic sheets, practised our navigation and fieldcraft and began to learn some of the most basic skills of soldiering. I learnt how shell scrapes were dug in frozen earth to protect us from artillery fire; how four-man fire teams worked together to gain ground on the enemy; and I also learned how much I hated the cold.

The drum beat of the General Purpose Machine Gun (GPMG) sounded from the distance as we patrolled towards the enemy position. This was Exercise Bayonet Point – live firing, Sandhurst style – and my heart was pumping with excitement. With only one kilometre left on our march it was impossible not to be mesmerized by the occasional beauty of warfare. Ahead of us, in a long Welsh valley – for the next few hours occupied by a Russian Motor Rifle company – was our prey. Soon, we would descend into the chaos of combat: layers of confusion, noise, adrenalin and fear; but now, for a few minutes at least, we could afford to enjoy the spectacle before us.

Brief muzzle flashes lit individual firers a fraction of a second before bright red tracer arced like refracted light through the pitch black night, its lazy, looping trajectory in stark contrast to the hellish effect it had on its goal, smashing through sand bags, bricks and wooden targets. This elegant light show was interrupted every few seconds as a round struck a rock and ricocheted straight upwards, reaching for the sky, before the tracer burned out and disappeared from view.

The light of a 51mm illumination mortar hung over the battlefield for a few seconds as the detonation of PE4 explosive echoed around the valley. We were now much closer: only 200 metres to go and the smell of smoke and cordite had rolled down the valley to our holding area. In a few minutes we would be unleashed, would storm up the valley with barely time to think before regrouping at the other end.

'All this and you get fucking paid, too, gentlemen.' Colour Sergeant Hupp stood directly behind the platoon drawing the acrid smell of gunpowder into his lungs. Only a Guardsman could patrol 10 kilometres and still look immaculate. 'Now get ready. This is the closest you are going to get to war until you find yourself in some godforsaken shithole somewhere. Take it in, learn from it and . . .' (he leaned forward, out of sight of the other Sandhurst Directing Staff who hovered nearby, and lowered his voice) 'fucking enjoy it.'

The valley had rested between platoons, but now, as a Sch-ermuly flare erupted into the night and we were launched forward, it filled with life again. The rattle of SA80 rifles pierced my eardrums as men to my left and right engaged the enemy and loosed off long bursts into the darkness. Fire teams sprinted forward into that darkness and were covered by huge weights of fire from elsewhere in the platoon.

Bayonets that until this week had been used exclusively on the parade ground now glinted in the fraction of a second before they were pushed, with real, poisonous rage, into sand-filled mannequins. Exercise or not, this was terrifying stuff: live rounds, real people in the darkness, with GPMGs spewing fire above and to our sides as PE4 plastic explosives detonated all around us.

I was struck by the ironies of combat: how could it be that so much was shouted but so little understood? How can so many bright men make such a hash of something we expect people with little or no education to do perfectly every time? Why did the loudest, most outgoing men in the platoon withdraw into themselves during this chaos? What was the difference between the men and women who could handle this kind of anarchy and those that were immediately overwhelmed by it?

Apart from my hatred of the cold I had learned something else on exercise: I liked it. I loved the mayhem and confusion of battle and managed to keep a clear head when others seemed to buckle. My secret, as yet unspoken to my Platoon Commander or even close friends, was that I wanted to find that kind of action again. I wanted to find war.

In the rare moments at Sandhurst when we were not either on the parade ground or on exercise, lectures were given on contemporary military operations and on leadership. Bosnia, Kosovo and Northern Ireland provided the context for instruction and we sat open mouthed as videos of the Balkans and Northern Ireland played on the huge screens in front of us.

I watched as British Warrior armoured fighting vehicles were blown up by anti-tank mines and as our soldiers came under fire from militia dug into snow-covered hilltops – all to the tune of Dire Straits 'Brothers in Arms'.

The soldiers screaming in agony on the huge screen before me could have been me, my friends, my father. The emotional attachment to soldiers forged in my early childhood magnified tenfold the horror of seeing British soldiers in distress. I wanted to get out there so much that it hurt. I wanted to 'do my bit', to *make a difference*.

As we marched around the Old College parade ground, the sound of 'Highland Cathedral' played by the pipes and drums of the Royal Scots added an inch to our stride and allowed the tension of the Commissioning Course to ebb away. Slow marching up the Old College Steps to 'Auld Lang Syne', I wondered whether all the theory or the hours shivering in Sennybridge Training Area would ever be put into practice. The Army had troops in Northern Ireland and the Balkans, but there seemed little possibility of a Falklands or Gulf War in the near future.

Immediately after the course I was plunged into my first real taste of the Army. As a troop commander at 29 Regiment RLC I led a troop of twenty Movement Controllers. To be a 'Mover' was to be that most loathed of military creatures: not only was he responsible for operating airports, seaports, railheads and acting as a paramilitary travel agent, he was also responsible for transmitting the errors, failures and incompetence of the RAF to the many thousands of soldiers who required their services.

But regimental life was everything I had ever dreamed of: sport was frequent, Friday afternoons always free and I quickly discovered that I loved dealing with soldiers. Simultaneously exasperating, brilliant and always challenging, I enjoyed nothing more than leading men and women.

Although much time was spent away on exercise, life in camp had many benefits. The Officers' Mess was superb fun for a young officer but I, like every other new subaltern, would not be welcomed into the mess until I had passed its bizarre induction ceremony. I soon found myself being placed on top of a 6-feet high set of Jenga and having an evil multicoloured concoction poured into a plastic glass and thrust into my shaking hands.

As I balanced precariously on top of the swaying tower, drunken hands slowly, clumsily, pulled pieces away as onlookers howled loudly. Before long, gravity had won the day and I came crashing down, legs and arms at peculiar angles, slightly winded, before another drink was thrust into my hand and the tower rebuilt. It was a healthy regiment, morale was high and in between periods overseas a fantastic atmosphere reigned in the mess. Life was great; as far as I was concerned the recruiting brochures had been spot on!

However, one September day the atmosphere changed. I walked into the Officers' Mess TV room and noted a scrum of people sitting on chairs, the floor and standing still at the back. The room was silent, tepid mugs of tea held in hands that remained motionless, and cigarettes burnt to their end, unsmoked. Eyes were transfixed by the images that flashed across the screen in front of us; the same footage replayed again and again. Heads slowly shook as we began to understand the enormity of the events playing out before us. It wasn't just the images of the airliner flying into the tower that had shocked us all, it was seeing people jumping to their deaths. Talking heads and news broadcasters espoused a myriad of theories as to the perpetrators, the casualties and the reason for the attack. That day – 11 September 2001 – would change the world, the British Army and my life dramatically, even if at that time I had little idea exactly how.

I knew only one thing for sure. We were going to war.

*

By November, UK forces had secured a foothold in Afghanistan and images of the Special Boat Service (SBS), who had taken Bagram airfield, north of Kabul, from the Taliban, filled the news. I scented my opportunity. I lobbied hard and wide that I should be the one to lead the movements team into Afghanistan. Other than my enthusiasm there was no compelling reason why I should have been selected above my contemporaries, but it worked. I finally left camp at midnight on 31 December 2001. Big Ben chimed over the radio as we boarded the bus to Brize Norton, where we were to board the C-130 that would take us to Afghanistan.

Moments after bumping down on to the runway in Kabul, the tail ramp of the C-130 opened and the smells of Kabul rushed in, cloaking us with the tang of smoke that hung low across the city, colouring the air and marking our faces. Artificial lights lit up long deserted relics of the Afghan/Soviet conflict in every corner of the airfield. Taking centre stage, the rear third of a Boeing 747 lay stricken in the centre of the taxi area; behind it, the terminal had been perforated with small arms fire and was testament to the ferocity of the fighting during the occupation. Overhead, a procession of American B-2 bombers, which constantly pounded Taliban positions, was returning to base.

The mountain ranges, on top of which the silhouettes of rusting tanks and artillery pieces were still clearly visible, loomed out of the darkness. I had struck gold, finding conflict within a year of commissioning and in one of the most beautiful countries on the planet.

Although we had little food, no heating and only solar showers that had to be thawed during the day to be used, morale was high and the days long and rewarding. Frequent meetings at the International Security and Assistance Force (ISAF) HQ in the centre of the city meant that fascinating daily trips through the centre of Kabul became routine. Although the country was at war, the city was lively and seemed never to slow. The markets that sold bread, stews and spices battled with each other for local custom, while the rug, antique and jewellery sellers jostled for the attention of the many foreigners who rolled around the city in 4 x 4 vehicles and lived in an opulence that few Afghans could imagine.

Most Afghans I spoke to were as polite, hospitable and friendly as any people I have ever met. They were as interested in my culture as I was in theirs and during my down time I would walk to the small market outside the airport and talk of Afghan history and the Soviet occupation with anyone I could find. In addition to their pleasantness, many Afghans shared another trait: fatigue. They were tired of war, tired of death and tired of their country's constant occupation. They delighted in reminding me that this was not the first time the British had been here and said that they hoped we would have more success this time.

Upon my return to the UK I found that I had been selected to attend the ATO course starting in November. I was overjoyed to have passed another hurdle on my way to becoming a bomb disposal operator and even happier when I saw that six other members of my Troopies course had also been selected. Amongst the prospective ATOs were Charlie Yorke, who had arrived at Sandhurst after working in the family engineering business and seemed about as focused an individual as any on the course. Then there was Mickey Eason, a bluff Northerner who was an atypical Sandhurst Officer cadet with his deep Yorkshire accent, and Carl Newsome, a good-looking Scot who was quiet, worked out religiously and was as nice a man as you could wish to meet.

As I arrived at the Royal Military College of Science, Shrivenham (RMCS or 'Shriv') in November 2002, ready to be handed my pliers, night vision goggles and black overalls, I eyed the fellow students in the way a boxer does at the weigh-in. We would spend the sixteen months of the course living together, working together and ultimately fighting for the same jobs, with the better performing students having their pick of the best.

To my slight disappointment, the first six months comprised mainly academic instruction on maths, physics and chemistry in addition to more applied lessons on explosive technology. Hours were spent crawling over Russian tanks and inside helicopters as we began to understand how armies used technology to kill each other.

It quickly became apparent that there were two types of ATO. The 'Depot Donkeys' who passed the ATO course but failed the Improvised Explosive Device Disposal (IEDD) section tended to spend their careers managing ammunition supply and storage, whereas the 'Bomb Gods' who passed the IEDD phase were posted to 11 Explosive Ordnance Disposal (EOD) Regiment. These were the guys and girls who whizzed around the country with blue lights flashing as they dashed from incident to incident, defusing anything from Second World War hand grenades to terrorist bombs.

Only the latter group, the Bomb Gods, would be destined for great things within the ATO world. It was this group alone that could attend the 'High Threat' IEDD course and only the very few successful candidates (only about 20 per cent passed) would deploy to Northern Ireland to take on the most sophisticated IED threat in the world at the time: that posed by the Provisional IRA. No one would choose to be a Depot Donkey and each of us fixed our eyes on the prize of being a Bomb God.

Now, at the very beginning of the ATO course and having already passed several hurdles to reach this point, the chance of becoming a bomb disposal operator seemed more distant than ever. I was determined to focus on work and work alone for the next sixteen months. The rewards were too great for me to focus on anything else; the sacrifice would be worth it.

Then I met Beth. My friend Jack and I were celebrating buying a flat together when he looked across the bar and recognized two girls with whom he had been to school. Armed with a bottle of Moet et Chandon and the confidence of inebriation we sidled across. Before introductions were over I was already smitten with Beth. She was everything I wanted in a woman: very good looking, funny, independent and fiercely intelligent. By the end of the night, we had agreed to meet for dinner and I had already started to fall in love with her. She was studying at Oxford University, only a short trip from Shrivenham, and we spent afternoons enjoying picnics at Christ Church College or walking through the winding paths that snaked alongside the Isis, itself teeming with young couples punting up and down the river.

By the time I left Shrivenham, Beth and I were already deeply in love and my thoughts began to waver from chasing the all-action postings that I had imagined to more stable jobs where I could spend more time with Beth, building a life together. But it was no good. Even as the course progressed my desire to see war up close grew greater and greater. Surely I didn't have to choose between Beth and the Army. Surely I could have both. Besides, I wanted to do tough exciting tasks. I wanted her to be proud of me.

As the next phase of the ATO course began at the Army School of Ammunition in Banbury, I worked far harder than I ever had at school or college and soon I was a walking encyclopaedia of ammunition facts. I was far from being the brightest on the course, but no one worked harder than me and from a dismal start my name began to creep up the all-important rankings which, along with the IEDD course, would determine our postings.

Meanwhile my relationship with Beth was bliss. We had started to plan together, to talk about the future. She was heading for a Magic Circle law firm in London, I was doing well on the ATO course and would probably be able to choose my posting. And as there was one available in London, everything seemed set.

Not a single day went by without me telling her I loved her. Nothing made me happier than simply holding her hand and looking into her eyes. We were infatuated and I knew that I had her support in my role as an ATO. I would go to London for two years and gain some experience, pass the High Threat course, deploy to Northern Ireland and then aim for the role as ATO to the Special Forces. For the first time in my life there was a plan, and I could not think of a better person to spend my life with.

The IEDD course was the very last phase of the ATO course. Everything hung on it, to the extent that we would receive our postings the day we finished the phase. If we passed, we would probably go to 11 EOD Regiment; if we failed, a life of counting ammunition boxes awaited. The thought of not passing was unbearable. As we arrived at the Felix Centre for our five-week course, we were under no illusions as to how important IEDD was to our future careers.

'99 per cent boredom and 1 per cent terror.' Captain Doug Gregory stood before us, a veteran of over twenty-five years as an ATO. He had done it all: Northern Ireland, Special Forces and now Chief Instructor of the UK's counter-terrorist bomb disposal training school.

'Most of the time in this game you will be sat around doing sweet eff all, but when you are called you have to get it right every single time.'

This was our gentle introduction to bomb disposal. Fourteen faces looked stunned.

'But good luck and enjoy it.'

'No pressure then,' said a voice from the back after Doug had left the room. We laughed quietly and nervously.

Practical lessons followed the theory lessons on the principles and philosophies of IEDD, the role of each team member and the conduct of an IEDD task. The course wasted no time in sending us outside on practice tasks where we would deploy in teams within the small village constructed for the purpose. In amongst the many houses were pubs, petrol stations, a post office and even a car showroom.

On arrival, our priority was to establish what had happened, where it had happened and what had already been done about it. Scenarios, based on real tasks, ranged from dealing with simple incendiary devices like those constructed by animal rights groups, through to the most sophisticated devices the Provisional IRA had deployed in Great Britain. Although the explosives were not real, the pressure definitely was. Often we would arrive at a task only to find that we had been brought into an unsecured area where a secondary device had been placed to kill the bomb disposal team.

Tasks with secondary devices generally led to the death of the entire team: they were difficult, complex and required first class skills and intuition to overcome. I hoped that my time would come, that I would get to test myself for real and, most of all, that I would be equal to the challenge.

The final week was test week. There were four tasks, three of which we had to pass in order to qualify as IEDD operators. One by one my fellow students failed: some could not handle the pressure and just broke on task, some did not possess the technical skills to succeed and a few lacked the command skills to operate.

I passed.

Fifty per cent of the course had failed and would have to re-sit the course or accept their fates counting bullets. The relief was massive, as I was virtually assured of one of my top three postings in the UK with 11 EOD Regiment. I had made it. Beth was over the moon and it seemed as if my efforts had been worth it. Overall I had finished second on the ATO course and could not wait to receive my posting.

But on judgement day I was posted to Germany. I was considered too young to stay in the UK and was banished abroad. Beth was heartbroken, but we were doubly determined to make our relationship succeed.

In Germany, life in camp was straightforward, with few bomb disposal callouts and little prospect of the Soviet 3rd Shock Army rolling towards us at any time soon in order to shake things up. In addition to the welfare of my soldiers, one subject occupied my mind: the High Threat IEDD course. This course was extraordinarily difficult to pass and was the biggest hurdle between me and the sexier ATO jobs in Special Forces or Intelligence and my ticket to real action. The thought of spending two years in Germany waiting for the Provisional IRA to mount another attack depressed me; here I was, stuck in the middle of nowhere, while the Army engaged in two bloody conflicts thousands of miles away – which was where I wanted to be.

I had missed the second Iraq War due to the ATO course. In the ATO community there was much talk of our actions in Iraq. We had lost a Staff Sergeant early in the war when he had been killed defusing a cluster bomb, but we had been lucky since. 'High Threat' ATOs were already in theatre and I learned that in a town called Al Amarah, a war was raging. The Princess of Wales Royal Regiment Battle Group (PWRR Battle Group) were in the thick of the action and the ATOs were taking incredible risks against IEDs to keep the Battle Group alive.

I wanted in. I wanted to deploy immediately, and fantasized about passing the High Threat course and getting out there as soon as I could.

Not possessing a natural gift for IEDD, I trained hard to sharpen my skills and to soak up as much experience as I could before the High Threat course. However, my confidence took an extra dip as on day one, Captain Doug once again addressed us:

'The pass rate for this course is about 30 per cent, for those of you here for the first time it is about 20 per cent – but good luck.' This guy really had a way with words.

Beginning with instruction on searching for sophisticated booby traps and using complex 'hook and line' arrangements to remove mortars from culverts and wheelie bins dug into the ground, the course was intense physically but less cerebrally demanding. We spent hours clambering through streams and up rivers, and wriggling through sewage pipes attaching ropes and pulleys to large main charges so that we did not have to remove them by hand. If we made a pattern of moving things ourselves, the enemy would booby trap them and kill us. It was important to achieve as much as possible whilst still keeping distance between ourselves and the bomb.

The course progressed to advanced search techniques. Looking for and disabling victim-operated devices was demanding and required hours spent in the claustrophobic EOD suit which restricted vision and movement and would protect us against only the smallest devices. Any more than a hand grenade and we would certainly die if we were close up. We learnt how to search for metal IEDs dug in beside railway tracks, under concrete floors and in all environments: urban, rural, dry and wet, both at night and by day.

Gradually our skills were put into use in practice tasks with one member from each team being tested as his colleagues looked on. On one occasion I had finished my task – a simple command wire to a high explosive main charge – and was clearing up. The DS – our instructor – stood by longer than usual and more gathered nearby as I wound in the command wire. I pulled and pulled until I felt it snag. Then from the leaves piled 20 metres away I realised I had been pulling a second main charge, an artillery shell, towards me for the last few minutes.

'We'll call that a fail and chalk it up as a good lesson to learn,' said Staff Sergeant Davis, stifling his laughter as the bomb rolled slowly towards me.

Despite this explosive faux pas I passed the course and was now a qualified High Threat bomb disposal operator. This was my ticket to the action, to what I'd always dreamed of. Beth, however, seemed much less happy.

'You passed? That's great news for *you*.' I barely noticed her concern as I gathered my kit and prepared to deploy to Northern Ireland. I had focused so intently on my career that I had not seen how our relationship was breaking apart. We were rarely together, and when we were I thought only of making the grade as a High Threat operator.

If I had spent more time thinking about her it would have come as no surprise when, only two weeks into my deployment, Beth ended our two-year relationship. It was just too difficult for her. I lived in Germany and would spend the next six months in Londonderry as she built a life in London. We spent too much time apart and she needed more. Before I put the phone down she had tried to soften the blow.

'I love you and if you ever need me I will always be there for you.'

As I stared out of the window, I knew my life had been turned upside down. The plans, ambitions and life I thought we would have together were no more. I had chased my ambitions too hard and had lost the girl I loved because of it.

Not long afterwards, petrol bombs lit up the Londonderry night as stones turned my EOD van into a bass drum. We were being hammered. This crowd hated us, hated the police and did not care that the pipe bomb I was hunched over had been meant for them. A female PSNI officer had been attacked with a golf club seconds earlier and my own team was sheltering in the van as flames licked all around the road.

I lifted my visor, took in the scene and smiled. I was the ATO in Londonderry and had been tasked to Strabane at 3 a.m. in the morning. Seven years ago this area would have been covered by the ATO Omagh. I had made it. A brick skidded along the floor and struck me in the shin as I knelt. I didn't care. I was living my dream.

However, only a few days later my phone rang and it was Keith, my boss from Germany, sounding as chirpy as ever.

'I've got a bit of a proposition for you, one I think you may like.'

My ears pricked up.

'What would you say if I offered to cut short your Northern Ireland tour and get you out to Iraq? You would do four months in each theatre.'

I was enjoying every second of my time in Northern Ireland. There was nothing more exhilarating than charging through the city defusing pipe bombs, getting petrol bombed and returning to the PSNI bar to wind down. This was everything I had wanted ever since my first visit to Omagh all those years ago. But there was really no decision to make.

'I'd bite your fucking hand off.'

2. ATO AL AMARAH

I could barely hide my smile as the Merlin helicopter swept effortlessly over the desert towards Al Amarah, my home for the next four months. The heli was packed with a dozen soldiers; some had collapsed into exhausted sleep before we had even taken off in Basra, some had pulled worn-out paperbacks from the top pouch of their rucksacks and escaped the war by thumbing, for a few precious minutes, through stories from another place, and some, like me, were so excited that it was all we could do not to dance a jig as we flew.

The Merlin was thundering towards the action I had dreamt of constantly in the six years since I had first met ATO Omagh. If I couldn't find adventure as the sole bomb disposal man in the most dangerous town in Iraq, I never would.

Strapped to the floor of the heli was our kit: a huge pile of rucksacks, day sacks and army grip bags mixed with belts of 7.62mm bullets, rifle grenades and boxes of red phosphorous smoke grenades. Whatever our level of consciousness, each of us wore our webbing, brimming with ammunition, water and first aid supplies, our helmets, marked with our name and blood group, and clutched our rifles adorned with newly issued laser pointers, torches and push-to-talk radio transmitters on the grip stock.

Most of my fellow passengers had clearly been in theatre for

38

some time and looked exhausted. Their faces were lined with deep furrows of fatigue and darkened by the thin layer of sand that coated everyone, the same dull yellow as the desert rushing below us. Even their webbing was barely recognizable, due to the amount of additional material added to it: from the sand coloured paint, to personal details such as name, rank and number, and a range of extra pouches crammed with high explosive fragmentation grenades and First Field Dressings. These older hands stared blankly ahead and said little, the lack of fire or energy in their eyes in stark contrast to the uncontainable nervous energy that bubbled over in us new-comers. The heli stank of stale sweat and the generic army smell which somehow emanated from everything: tanks, tents, buildings, everything.

My uniform was new, shiny, ironed and unblemished, my hair conspicuous in its cleanliness and the gentle aroma of shampoo. Even my rifle gleamed in the Iraqi light from its careful maintenance and delicate application of gun oil. Tired eyes opened briefly and looked at me with pity and no small amusement as I constantly adjusted my collar, not yet used to the harsh Iraqi climate that burned through the Merlin's windows. The heat was so claustrophobic and intense that breathing became so much harder, like breathing at altitude.

At the back of the heli the door gunner was itching for a fight, constantly swinging the barrel of his GPMG left to right across huge swathes of desert, his finger dancing nervously on the trigger. I felt sorry for any Bedouin tribesmen under our flight path: one false move, one poorly timed look at the heli and Dirty Harry would let rip. Even the goats on the ground seemed to sense the door gunner's edginess and looked down at the ground, inspecting their feet.

The Bedouin were right to be cautious. They knew better than anyone the military history of southern Iraq. For far too long, Al Amarah had stood on a historical fault line, one which had erupted into violence so often that the people knew of little else.

Al Amarah had been in a state of almost constant conflict throughout the twentieth century because of its strategically important position near the Iranian border and the Tigris and Euphrates rivers. Established in the 1860s as an Ottoman military outpost, the town had been captured and garrisoned by the British in the summer of 1915. A British cemetery still stood in the north of the town, a reminder to Brits and locals alike that this was not the first time British Forces had been stationed there.

The town itself has a population of just over 400,000 and lies halfway between Basra and Baghdad, 10 kilometres north of the poisonous town of Al Majar Al Kabir, known as Al Mak. It was here that six Royal Military Policemen had been murdered in June 2003 and it was now an area where British forces rarely ventured. Al Mak was like Mogadishu in *Black Hawk Down*.

Dissecting Basra, Al Amarah, Al Mak and Baghdad was the coalition's Main Supply Route (MSR), Route 6. This road and the town's isolated position between the major cities of Baghdad and Basra make it the ideal artery for trade in all manner of materials from bricks to silver to weapons.

Only 50 kilometres to the east of Al Amarah was the Iranian border, its proximity the reason for the town taking the full force of the Iran/Iraq conflict of the 1980s. Even now the border was littered with the remnants of the war, including armoured vehicles, artillery pieces and minefields. These were more than the curious legacy of a bygone conflict; the minefield provided a ready stock of raw material for the modern insurgents who dug up the mines, harvested the high explosive and manufactured IEDs when supplies of C4 explosive from Iran were low.

Al Amarah had also seen some of the most ferocious fighting since the latest ground war started in 2003, with the price of its occupation being paid in blood. This was the town where Private Johnson Beharry cheated death so many times and was awarded a Victoria Cross, where Beharry's Battle Group, the PWRR, had undertaken the incredible defence of CIMIC (Civil-Military Co-operation) house and where British soldiers had fixed bayonets and charged the enemy at the Battle of Danny Boy.

The key to our presence in Al Amarah during this war was the same as it was in the previous wars.

Iran.

The coalition had lost countless lives and taken thousands of casualties due to the weapons supplied by the Iranian regime to our enemies in Iraq. The flood of explosives, IEDs and conventional weapons from Iran along Route 6 and to all corners of the country was critical in supporting the Shia insurgency that had replaced conventional Iraqi forces when the Iraqi army had been so easily swept aside during the war proper.

The 107mm high explosive Katyusha rockets that peppered UK forces in Al Amarah and Basra every night, and the infamous Explosively Formed Projectiles (EFPs) which had repeatedly punctured lightly armoured coalition vehicles, were manufactured in Iran and supplied by the Iranian Revolutionary Guard Corps (IRGC) to the Mahdi army and other Shia groups who were so determined to kick the occupiers out of Iraq.

Al Amarah was the first stop on the bomb-makers' route from Iran to Baghdad and acted as a useful testing ground as they perfected their IED designs.

As we sped towards camp I peered out of the small window beside me. Desert had given way to luscious forestry and the winding River Tigris which snaked through the heart of Al

Amarah. Marketplaces bustled beneath me as I looked at the horizon, where smoke stacks billowed from tiny brick factories.

Below us, laundry strained on string lines strewn between buildings and mini dust storms erupted as the rotors spun into a blur. Feral dogs eyed us suspiciously before continuing with their business and chickens were briefly blown off their feet before dragging themselves up and padding about their cages. As we swooped over small villages, children stopped playing and stared up at us before breaking into huge smiles, waving as they blinked in the intense sunlight.

The gunner waved back, a brief respite from his hunt for trigger time.

Their parents appeared, unarmed, dragging their children back inside and frowning at us. They were definitely not excited by our presence.

The heli pilots chatted constantly on the net.

'Wires 400 metres dead ahead.' The heli ascended slightly.

'Tower 800 north west,' as a smoke stack billowed smoke into the air in front of us.

'Lynx Zero Charlie dead ahead!' An Army helicopter passed across our front some distance away.

Suddenly we dropped.

I felt weightless as we hurtled toward the ground. My hands gripped each side of the seat and my whole body tensed.

Was this it? Were we going in? I had seen no smoke trails from an RPG or a Surface to Air Missile (SAM), no bullets had pierced the heli and no alarms sounded, but still we fell. This wasn't a controlled fall, this was the real deal, some mechanical failure had caused the heli to fail and we were dropping like a stone. I braced, knuckles turning white as the Tigris filled more and more of the window, the horizon disappearing from view altogether. There had been no explosion, no collision that I had heard or seen and yet the ground got closer and closer.

'FUCKING HELL!' We were moments away from striking the ground and I could not contain myself.

Then we levelled out. I opened one eye, then two and looked up.

As I looked around at my fellow passengers, some of whom had barely glanced up from their bestsellers and many of whom were still asleep. I caught the eye of one, a grizzled veteran who had undoubtedly made this journey many times before. He winked and gave me the thumbs up. Later I would find out that helicopters drop so quickly near landing and soar upon take-off to avoid incoming fire from machine guns and missiles.

Readjusting my collar, I checked around the heli to see if anyone else had noticed my panic. The ear-piercing whirr of the engine had drowned out any noises I made and no one else seemed to have noticed me bracing for impact. I had escaped both death and humiliation in a few seconds.

The horizon reasserted itself in my window as we raced along the river. We were low, only 30 metres or so above the water, which rippled as the pressure from the rotors hammered down. Dead ahead I could see a stationary column of armoured vehicles surrounded by low yellow buildings.

Even here, some distance from the centre of the town, traffic was everywhere, cars nose to tail on Route 6 and the road junctions to small villages nearby. Here was a city trying to repair itself and improve the lives of its residents. It seemed vibrant, like a much less beautiful, much more dangerous Kabul.

As the heli slowed, my home for the next four months, Camp Abu Naji, appeared below us. It was an incredible sight: only 300 by 800 metres, it occupied a disused Iraqi army barracks which was rumoured to have stored chemical weapons in the Gulf War only 7 kilometres south of Al Amarah. Now I could see that it comprised no more than a dozen single-storey stone buildings which blended into the yellowness of the surrounding desert, half a dozen portakabins and two huge metal structures underneath which men crawled over Challenger 2 tanks.

The pilots pointed out two 20-metre high arches which acted as gateways to the camp from Route 6.

'The Golden Arches,' the co-pilot said over the intercom.

'The moment you pass them on the way into town expect to get fucked up. That stretch of road is IED and RPG central.'

I fumbled with the A3 spot map I had stored in my pocket and could see that the Golden Arches stood only 200 metres east of camp: 200 metres of safety and then we should start expecting incoming.

'Fuuuck.' The squeal of the Merlin rotors provided all the anonymity I needed; no one could hear my involuntary cursing. This really was war.

To the north of camp I could just pick out the expanse of concrete that my map indicated was an airfield named Sparrowhawk. The Tigris river we had been tracing lay to the east of camp some 100 metres beyond the arches and wound lazily through the centre of town. Dotted all around the area were ammunition stores that had been levelled by air-dropped munitions during the initial stages of the war, or demolished by the first UK troops in the area to reduce the supply of military explosives falling into enemy hands. It hadn't worked. Car bombs in this part of the world were manufactured primarily from old ordnance looted from these stores; the insurgents were as well armed as the Iraqi army had been.

Even as the Merlin circled to land into the wind I could hear the grunt of a Challenger 2 dragging its 72 tonnes of armour around camp and the whine of Sea King helicopters preparing for take-off. At the front gate, soldiers crouched under trees, finding some brief respite from the heat before jumping in to the back of a very un-air-conditioned Warrior or Snatch vehicle for an eight-hour patrol. Happier looking soldiers ran around the edge of camp in PT kit, relishing every moment out of uniform and away from their heavy body armour. Everyone carried water: the heat would not forgive anyone who did not drink enough.

At the centre of camp I saw staff officers hurriedly running between offices carrying stacks of paper. Uniform was functional: there were no parades, no inspections and no sergeant-majors walking around with sticks here. Everywhere I looked, soldiers' unironed shirts were hanging out and webbing had been modified to accept extra magazines, more water or extended first aid kits.

The Royal Scots Dragoon Guards Battle Group comprised two companies of Highlanders with their Warriors, a squadron of Scots DGs equipped with Challenger 2 tanks and a company from the 2nd Battalion The Parachute Regiment armed only with the knowledge that they were the toughest, most fearless soldiers in the world. Parachute Regiment soldiers all wore kneepads and were built like Roman gladiators, the Scots DGs wore grubby overalls for use inside their tanks and the young Jocks of the Highlanders had ditched their elegant Tam o' Shanters for much more functional berets. Apart from those running around camp everyone had body armour, helmet, a First Field Dressing bandage (FFD), morphine and a cyalume light stick hanging from them.

Only two months into a six-month tour, the Battle Group was eager, motivated, well armed and already blooded. Young men, officers and NCOs had led patrols into some of the most dangerous neighbourhoods in the world and had come out on top in every single contact.

Crucially, the Battle Group reserved violence for the most extreme situations. Its success would not be measured by how many kills it achieved or how much of downtown Al Amarah it turned into rubble, but by its ability to provide security for reconstruction projects and stop the flow of lethal weapons from the east. The UK had no stomach for a total war here, although many Battle Groups had come close since the first coalition forces had entered Al Amarah.

As we landed and the rotors began to slow, I could see a queue of Warriors waiting patiently at the main gate. Five vehicles would contain about fifty men. I imagined them in the back, cradling their SA80s and looking forward to the pneumatic door springing open in town to escape the suffocating, stifling heat of the Warrior. As I watched they disappeared, leaving only a huge dust storm and deep track marks. Turrets swivelled back and forth, commanders appeared at the top hatch and drivers poked their heads up at the front left of the vehicle, next to the engine. The familiar roar of the Perkins Rolls-Royce engine receded as the Warriors sped towards the town.

The camp was spartan, devoid of any luxury whatsoever and reminded me of pictures of South Armagh in the 1970s and 80s. This was soldiering at its purest. We had nothing except ourselves, our fighting equipment and a sophisticated enemy whom we respected and who had the capability to do us real harm. Basra already seemed a world away with its Pizza Hut, Starbucks and bars. We were the lucky ones; no one wanted to be stuck in a world of pointless parades, doing the same 9 to 5 job that they did back in Germany or the UK.

Al Amarah was the front line.

As the wheels of the Merlin touched down, a smile spread across my face, I realized I had found what I'd been looking for.

I was home.

3. IN ROUTINE

21 November – 27 February 2006

Ninety-nine per cent boredom, 1 per cent terror. My mind drifted back to my instructors laughing as they described life in a counter-terrorist bomb disposal team. I could put up with the 99 per cent boredom, but it was the 1 per cent terror I was after.

In Al Amarah my team and I were on standby, ready to deploy at a moment's notice, 24 hours a day, seven days a week, for four months. The vast majority of the time we were idle, waiting, training, and waiting some more. However, our world could turn from agonizing boredom to indescribable horror in a matter of seconds. One phone call from the Ops room and we would burst out of camp and into action.

My anticipation and excitement at the thought of these tasks was muted only by the thought that when the call did come, someone else, some British soldier, had already been scared, hurt or killed. This grim fact hung constantly over my hopes to see conflict, but not enough to dent my appetite for action.

My second-in-command and the Number Two operator of the team, Jay Smallwood, and I had worked together in Northern Ireland and our friendship crossed the divide that would normally separate a captain and a corporal. Only a year younger than me, Jay was also born in Shropshire and had a cheeky sense of humour and laughter that was infectious, echoing around our accommodation at all hours.

47

Styling himself as a Mexican bandit, Jay had decided to sport a shaved head and droopy moustache for the length of the tour, his shiny head protected from the sun by the thin brimmed worn-out combat hat that served as cloth, sunshield and discus when unsuspecting backs were turned.

Presumably because he left school at 16, Jay never considered himself to be anything other than a rough, tough squaddie, but his intelligence and leadership skills sang out at anyone who met him. He was one of the most naturally gifted soldiers I had ever met, a man who epitomized the very best of the British soldier: loyal, dedicated and absolutely fearless. The kind of guy you would plead to be near if bullets started cracking overhead or men began to fall at your side. I had already been in Iraq for a month when Jay deployed and I had begged, fought and demanded that he come to my team. He was the best Number Two operator in the Army and was unlikely to be needed as much in Basra or Al Muthana. My Battle Group was at war and I wanted Jay by my side.

Jay and I belonged to 921 Explosive Ordnance Disposal (EOD) Squadron in Germany as did my Bleep, Corporal Terry 'Fitzy' Fitzgerald. Unlike Jay and me, whose lives consisted only of the Army, Fitzy had three passions in life: his wife and children always coming first, with soldiering and religion jostling for second place.

With thick, bushy sideburns, a slightly too long shaggy mop of hair, hands constantly thrust deep into pockets and a cigarette perched continually between his lips, Fitzy was the scourge of the sergeant majors who stalked around the camp. The self-styled 'God's Rottweiler' had more operational experience than any of us, had seen action in Iraq on many occasions and was also formidably bright. Fitzy's job was apparently simple: to stop me getting blown up by radio-controlled bombs.

A unique bond develops between ATO and Bleep. For those

minutes when I was walking down the road, I placed my life and my future in the hands of someone else. In the back of his van, Fitzy would furiously track incoming attack signals from amongst the flotsam of radio frequency traffic, block them and let me live another day. Alone amongst the vast arrays of brightly lit, bleeping green boxes, he was my single line of defence against bombs initiated by phones, radios and even electronic car-door openers.

It was simple: if he was good enough I would survive to see another day; if he failed, I would join so many other ATOs on the wall of remembrance at the Felix Centre, another plaque mounted on an all-too crowded wall.

He was the best in the business.

My weapons intelligence specialist, Corporal Claire Vogel, was fiery, professional and as tough as anybody in the Battle Group. She ran her intelligence operation in Al Amarah with an iron rod. Like most RMP she was very intelligent and knew her subject inside out. We needed her to be good; her work was responsible for putting some of the most prolific bomb-makers in Iraq behind bars or on the wrong end of a Special Forces Diemaco rifle. It was her reports that were crucial in linking incidents, IEDs and bombers and enabled us to strike back at the Shia groups who killed more British soldiers every week.

The 1,000 men in camp who almost all tried their luck with her found that beneath the pleasant, attractive veneer lay a temper that could terrify the hardest paratrooper and the toughest marine. Claire was in Iraq to do a job and anyone who thought for a second that she would be impressed by Para wings, cheeky chat or war stories soon found out that she had done just as much soldiering as any of them – and had probably done it better, too.

Like me, Jay, Fitzy and Claire volunteered to come to Iraq and be part of a bomb disposal unit, had a nose for adventure and knew exactly what they were getting into. They performed the most dangerous job in one of the most dangerous towns in the world, always putting other soldiers' lives before their own and I loved them for it.

Even when not deployed we would not waste the day, instead spending our time training the Battle Group in IED recognition, 'Actions On' encountering an IED and advising on drills to avoid IEDs altogether in elaborate 'Lanes of death' that we constructed on the long road between EOD House and the RAF Fire Section. The road was filled with all manner of inert ordnance hidden in rocks, under piles of earth, on top of trees and camouflaged in insulation foam. Platoon by platoon the Battle Group patrolled along the lanes and honed their IED recognition skills.

My whole team loved every minute we spent training the Battle Group and took great pride that no one had been seriously injured by an IED on our watch, never mind killed. The troops loved it too, they could relax, talk about bombs for an hour and know that every minute they spent training with my team made them safer outside the wire.

It was also a fantastic excuse for me to avoid the endless bureaucracy that poured down from the Royal Engineer-led EOD Group which seemed hell bent on crippling my team with nugatory administration. Back in Basra, at Shaiba Logistic Base or 'Sha-ibiza' they had the luxury of time, resources and sleep due to the much lower threat from rockets. We were just trying to stay sane and keep our colleagues alive.

So many reports had to be completed each week that I kept a separate checklist stapled to the EOD Ops wall to ensure I stayed up to date. Daily, weekly and monthly equipment checks, morphine, body armour and ID disc checks, ECM, secure telephone and radio checks were all carefully forged – and forwarded to Basra – even this seemed a full-time job.

My IEDD instructors had only been half right, I had seen the 1 per cent terror and the boredom but they never mentioned the 50 per cent bullshit.

While I spent inordinate amounts of time on trivial administration, no one seemed willing or able to help with the big issues. My EOD vehicle had developed a fault which would leave the Wheelbarrow robot dead for no apparent reason, my ECM often failed due to a faulty power lead and my EOD weapons were rotting after three years in the Iraqi desert. Dozens of email requests and long conversations with the EOD Group had produced no answers to these critical problems; my team, the Scots DGs and I were less safe because if it.

To top it all off neither the OC of the EOD Group nor the Ops Officer knew anything about IEDD or Counter-IED. Neither of them had a single qualification to their name in my field and yet they were calling the shots. Sometimes it seemed that there was no one in my chain of command between me and Tony Blair who had the slightest clue about contemporary bomb disposal operations. The group's Senior Ammunition Technician (SAT), John Hall, was vastly experienced but as a WO1 had a limited say in policy. At the Divisional HQ the SO2 EOD, Major Miles Lillywhite, had been sidelined due to some Royal Engineer politicking so now had no formal role with the EOD group or my chain of command.

A chain of command had been carefully constructed to keep anyone with knowledge of IED disposal away from appointments where they could save British and Iraqi lives.

But the rest of the Battle Group had it so much harder; every day they would patrol into hostile areas, each step bringing them closer to someone with a gun or a bomb, someone willing to take their own life in order to kill a British soldier. They did this day in, day out, without respite, for the most noble of reasons, not because they felt strongly that the conflict was just, nor because they believed wholeheartedly in our mission to reconstruct the town. They patrolled day after day because their friends did, it was dangerous and they wanted to help their muckers out.

The majority of us did believe in the mission. We were there to help the locals, each man trying daily to engage with the town's people, to find out how they could help, to try to deliver training, infrastructure and any other support they could. Theirs was an almost impossible task: to get to know the locals, to do everything they could to improve the lives of all citizens of Al Amarah and at the same time to protect themselves against the threat of snipers, IEDs and mob violence.

The Battle Group also had to be prepared to undertake one additional task: wreaking absolute carnage if they had to. The Challenger 2s were not here for show, and would be used to create hell if necessary. We asked young men to switch from mentor and teacher to brutal killer in the space of a few seconds and they never let us down.

Al Amarah was a prime example of the 'Three Block War', where within the space of three city blocks troops could be fighting, peacekeeping and delivering humanitarian relief. The same men had to switch from unleashing the 120mm high explosive rounds at enemy positions, to delivering food, within a single day, sometimes within just a couple of hours.

The buzz of living with an armoured Battle Group lengthened my stride and added to my smile as, every single day, I lived the dream I had held since the Army-awareness day in Preston. Never asleep, the camp bristled with life at every moment, front and rear gates constantly swung open as patrols returned dirty, exhausted and occasionally bloodied. In their place, fresh, showered, eager soldiers drove out at high speed towards Al Amarah or Al Mak and would not return for many hours, sometimes days.

The engines of Warriors and Challenger 2 tanks roared into

life throughout the day as the vehicles prowled slowly about the camp throwing up volumes of dust that would hang, apparently suspended in mid air, for a minute before being reinforced by the arrival of yet another tank. Taking any opportunity I could, I clambered around these beasts and talked to drivers and commanders about infrared sights, turrets and gun barrels. This was military porn writ large and I was in my element.

Above me, the bass thump of rotors and the metallic whine of the engines would penetrate the stifling heat and darkest night as Lynx, Sea King and Merlin helicopters ferrying troops and supplies around the battlespace passed overhead.

The biggest beasts, the Merlins, created so much downdraft that it was impossible to stand still when one landed near you; the huge scoops on the end of each rotor caused so much air turbulence that it was possible to lean forward and be supported by the force of the air rushing toward you. Along with this barrage of pressure came the machine-gun rattle of stones being thrown at super-high velocity due to the helicopter downdraft. Anyone within 50 metres would get a bit of the heli claymore; those who had been in camp for some time wore goggles and body armour permanently around the helipad. Anyone new made the mistake once, and after plucking small chips of rock from their flesh for an hour afterwards learned a valuable lesson.

The Lynx was smaller, more agile and with a lower payload but was unmatched in the thrill of flight. With the side door open and passengers buckled in, the heli could bank and give incredible views of the ground below, with nothing between observer and earth. It was impossible to hear anything from the town below as we circled, the sound of the rotors and our height above the town combining to give an eerie, voyeuristic feeling, like staring at the world's largest oil painting, through a faint yellow lens, the atmosphere permanently stained even at altitude. This surreal feeling of floating over a canvas gave a passenger no feeling of the terror and poverty below in Al Amarah.

As I returned from the shower each morning I would see large groups of Parachute Regiment soldiers running in groups around camp. They kicked up nearly as much dust as a Challenger 2, moved a lot more quickly and looked even more aggressive. At the front of the group, officers led the way, not for them the idea of standing at the side with a clipboard. The OC, Major Timewell, small, wiry and in his late thirties ran alongside Sergeant-Major Janner, a huge bald wrecking ball who looked every inch the Para. Half a step behind, the young platoon commanders must have wondered how on earth these old men could be at the front. Behind them, the very best of the army, the soldiers and NCOs of the Parachute Regiment encouraged, dragged and coerced every other member around the course.

The camp was small and anyone running around it completed at least three laps before retiring. As the Paras sprinted past the tall metal arches that acted as aiming markers for rocket attacks at the south-west corner of camp, they would see REME mechanics swarming around armoured vehicles, lifting engines from tanks and making minute alterations to sophisticated infrared sighting systems.

As the Para juggernaut passed Battle Group HQ, pallid staff officers emerged from their map-filled caves and squinted into the incessant sunlight that caused temperatures to rise to 55° in the summer and made travelling in a Warrior almost unbearable. These poor wretches were critical to the planning of the Battle Group's operations but spent much of their time poring over satellite images in dim offices and they relished the opportunity to get outside where they looked longingly at patrols leaving camp and platoon commanders returning from battle with their troops, filthy faces and war stories.

They appreciated more than most the cruel irony that all

Army officers face; as they gained battle-winning experience they became less and less likely to lead men into battle – the new blood from Sandhurst would spend his whole tour on the streets whilst the seasoned captain would spend much more time processing papers than he would with soldiers.

By the Hesco Bastion fortress that formed our front gate, the long queue of Locally Employed Civilians (LECs) stood patiently as each one was frisked, had his ID checked (they were all men) and was cleared to begin his day acting as interpreter, cleaner, DVD salesman or barber. They stood nervously, looking over their shoulders for unfamiliar Iraqi faces, as to work for the British in Iraq was a sin thought by many of their peers to be worthy of death. Most of them were here only because the $10 a day they got was too good an offer to miss.

Only a few of the LECs were spies, but every single one of them had a far greater understanding of the threat to camp than the entire Battle Group intelligence cell. It was possible to measure our life expectancies by the length of the LEC queue each morning; if none had turned up for work we could be sure that rockets would rain down on us that night; even $10 a day wasn't worth that risk.

Parked at the front gate with engines revving and soldiers poised to strike into action was the Quick Reaction Force (QRF). This platoon of men sat, slept and ate in a single large building awash with overused copies of *FHM* and *Nuts* stacked in foot high piles around the room, rarely left alone for enough time to gather dust. Their radio burbled constantly in the corner, a constant link to the Battle Group Ops room which would be their first indication of any action. If a patrol was in trouble, in a firefight or needed extra support for a risky task the QRF and its three Warriors would be out of the camp and sprinting towards the action within three minutes.

Life on QRF was a lot like life as an ATO; for the majority

of time people are happy when you are not being used, but when required you have to get it right every single time.

At the north-eastern corner of camp lay the insurgents' prime target and our most vulnerable area, the large tented accommodation that housed most of the Battle Group. Made up of straight rows of yellow domed tents, men and women slept twelve to a room, privacy afforded only by the thick mosquito net that covered each of the rickety metal beds and whatever sheets could be found and draped from the roof between bed spaces. Eight hundred souls lay still every night with nothing but the thin tent roof and luck protecting them from the intense heat, high pressure and supersonic fragmentation that accompanied every rocket falling on camp.

Within the accommodation was one of our few sanctuaries, our oases of calm and a precious link back to civilization, to what it was to be a human again. Showers allowed us to reconnect, to escape the nerves of conflict and re-establish a link with the people we were before we arrived in Al Amarah. Those few minutes when we could feel clean, before a helicopter flew overhead, a tank drove by or a gentle breeze deposited a thick film of sand covering us from head to toe once more, were heaven. Men and women frequently returned from the toughest of fire fights in Al Mak bloodied, traumatized and terrified, but after a shower, some food and a freshly bought DVD they could imagine that they were somewhere else for a few prized hours and be ready to soldier again.

The Camp Abu Naji canteen was constructed from eight portakabins linked together, filled with endless rows of plastic tables and chairs that squeaked along the ground with every movement. The same generic smell of army food had worn into the walls; the tang of fried eggs, chips and curry hung constantly in the air as did the hubbub of quiet conversation from every table.

To even enter the canteen each of us had to pass through the incredible stench that existed at the entrance caused, rumour told us, by the canteen being positioned above an ancient sewer. No wonder the barracks was deserted before we got there.

Newcomers to Camp Abu Naji retched when they got near. Older hands knew to hold their breath from 20 metres away and hurriedly washed their hands with increasingly blue faces before darting away from the door and into the queue for food, exhaling loudly in blissful relief.

North of the canteen, lame soldiers limped shamefully into the entrance of the medical centre to attend sick parade. Inside, the small waiting room saw troops thumbing through dated editions of *Soldier* magazine as doctors, nurses and physios walked purposefully, clutching patients' notes, prescriptions and 'biff chits', the red A5 notes that would excuse soldiers from specific activities for limited periods of time. The quiet efficiency of the med centre was shattered all too often as the Battle Group took casualties and med teams sprinted to waiting ambulances or helicopters carrying trauma bergans. The team of doctors were all very experienced medics who had chosen to ignore the opportunity of steady careers in the NHS or lucrative lives in private practice and were now with us in Iraq. They lived in the same dust, shared the same rocket attacks and lived with the same threat of death every day. And they performed miracles throughout the tour.

At the very centre of camp lay my home and office for four months: EOD House. My small single-storey building was unbelievable luxury compared to those housing the remainder of the Battle Group, and I had the prime spot, a tiny room to myself, after my predecessor had commandeered a disused shower and claimed it as his own. This was my haven of calm, my refuge from the stresses of work and it allowed me to keep some distance between me and my team on occasions when emotions ran high.

Although isolated from the main living areas, we were a little too close to the tankers full of aviation fuel for my liking but it was a solid building, and as the camp was frequently peppered with rockets, this provided some protection.

Nearby we had our explosives stores and the Aladdin's Cave where IEDs and other ordnance were stored after being rendered safe and before being obliterated by high explosive on our demolition days, when we took over one of the flattened ammo dumps nearby and evaporated as much ordnance as we could. Although often around 6 kilometres from camp the windows in the Battle Group Ops room would shake at each detonation and those of us much closer felt the blast pass through us as we sheltered in trenches and behind huge mounds of earth to protect us from shrapnel.

In addition to my room and the EOD Ops room, I spent much of my time sitting outside the house on a 500lb aircraft bomb that had been defused by previous occupants. Jay, Fitzy and I spent hours sitting on the 'Thinking Bomb' contemplating the issues of the day, bitching about the remainder of the Battle Group and watching the small tornadoes whisking up the film of sand that coated the road and depositing it over every exposed surface.

My team was close, far closer than most military units would find normal, and here on the Thinking Bomb rank seemed irrelevant, opinions were freely voiced and frustrations shared. It may not have been D-Day, Easy Company or even occupied France but my own Band of Brothers would gladly lay their own lives down for each other.

Each day I promised myself that whatever the task, whatever the chance of survival I would never put my team in more danger than me. I would do whatever I could to reduce the risk to them and if that meant taking more risk for myself, so be it.

At the end of each day I loved nothing more than to relax with my team and a can of Coke as the temperature dropped and the light faded. To our north, long streams of red and green tracer pierced the night like a macabre fireworks display as pitched battles were fought between rival militias, us and anyone else who fancied getting into the mix and loosing off their AK 47s.

Even in the absolute blackness of the Iraqi night, Jay and Fitzy were easy to spot; our collective inhalation and loud 'Shiiiiiiiit!' as the tracer shot into the sky caused the cigarettes that hung permanently from their mouths to glow even more brightly.

The combination of Army logisticians, engineers and the RAF made for an interesting mixture in EOD House. Although there was some overlap in skill sets there was also a definite hierarchy. The IEDD team, my team, sat at the top of the tree. Not only was our work the most technically difficult; it was also the most dangerous, high profile and high impact EOD capability the Battle Group possessed. When the Battle Group had an explosive-related problem of any kind, they turned to ATO – to me.

Below my team, the RAF CMD team conducted a lot of the tasks that my team could not afford to get bogged down with, such as mine clearance. They were excellent on technical explosives issues but had never been trained as soldiers and were therefore almost unemployable outside of the wire. It wasn't their fault – senior RAF officers had yet to notice that the world had changed since the Cold War and that front lines no longer existed.

The Royal Engineer Search Team (REST) did not conduct bomb disposal per se. Their operational role was to search for bombs dug into the road, hidden inside street furniture or camouflaged in kerb stones, expanded foam or even up trees.

In Northern Ireland I had been tasked to a find of six Mark 15 Barrack Buster mortars but could not find one of the propulsion units – a metal cylinder the size of a Pringles tube. I tasked the

REST to scour a large strip of shrubbery to find it and two men went on their hands and knees through every inch of it. You would think a steamroller had flattened the area after they had finished with it – and they found my propulsion unit, too. These guys were the best in the world.

Unfortunately for them, senior Royal Engineers were pressing for the REST and Engineer CMD team to take over more and more IEDD work – tasks that they were not recruited, trained or equipped to do. The teams knew they were not up to the job. I couldn't believe that senior officers would risk their own men's lives so unnecessarily.

Throughout the day, the slightest hint of anything explosive had me charging out of camp towards the target. Often these tasks were nothing more than the 'milk round', picking up recovered IED components and ordnance from the Iraqi Police. Within a week of arriving in Al Amarah, I was tasked to collect half a dozen mines at the Police Joint Operations Centre (PJOC), a three-storey building in the very heart of Al Amarah.

Led into town by the QRF of three Warriors, I was met at the PJOC by Captain Richard Holmes, the PJOC liaison officer. I had met Rich only briefly before but knew his reputation was first class; he lived and breathed the Iraqi lifestyle and spent his days mentoring the Iraqi police.

I leapt from the van and patted Rich on the back as he introduced me to Captain Maythan, the local police chief, both men looking at me in puzzlement as I strode towards the compound that they had indicated housed the mines. My bergan was open, ready to drop the mines into, and as I turned the corner toward the mines I heard raucous laughter behind me.

In front of me were six hundred anti-tank mines stacked in one corner of the concrete yard which so often acted as an explosives storehouse. Around 2 metres high and 2 metres wide, the pile was precarious. The mines were in varying states of deterioration and we had only a thin brick wall between us and the bullets which were exchanged so frequently on the road outside. This was a huge task that would require not only time but immense concentration as I defused each of the six hundred mines in turn. There would be no room for error whatsoever.

As I stood looking at the pile of ordnance in front of me I made my first mistake and looked at the bergan in my hand, a pitiful size compared to the mine mountain in front of me.

Over my shoulder Rich Holmes had seen me glance at the bergan and theatrically sucked his teeth, raised his eyebrows and exhaled loudly.

'Are you sure that bergan is big enough?' His smile widened as he looked on.

'Fuck off, Rich.'

'I mean, I'm no explosives expert or anything, I'm just a simple paratrooper but ...'

'Fuck off, Rich.'

By now, a small crowd of Iraqi policemen had closed in on Rich and howled loudly as I stood alone, helpless in front of over a tonne of high explosive.

'Let me get *my* bergan, that'll sort it.' Rich held his sides as all around him, the best and brightest of the Iraqi police force mimed trying to fit mines into a bag, standing back and scratching their heads as they looked down at imaginary rucksacks. The PRR clicked on and I spoke:

'Yeah guys, Jay, Fitzy can you reverse your vans around here. Claire, we may need more evidence bags.'

As the ECM van edged towards me, Jay appeared by my side, held out his hand and mimed counting the mines before looking puzzled and recounting.

'Well Capitano, that's not six, is it?'

As much as I would have loved to spite Rich and his crew of miming Iraqis, I knew I could not leave the mines in town.

Although little more than high explosive encased in plastic, it would take two minutes for them to be modified by any terrorist into a huge bomb that could level anything within 500 metres.

Three hours later my team and I had piled the mines into an armoured trailer and were driving through one of the most dangerous towns in the world, safe in the knowledge that a single stray RPG, bullet or grenade could detonate them all. The laughter that only hours earlier had rippled amongst us was forgotten as we edged slowly through the dense traffic, past houses, and finally out on to the open road that led back to camp.

Even once we were inside the perimeter we could not count on safety. If one of the many rockets that were fired at camp landed anywhere near my lethal cargo, there would no longer be a Scots DG Battle Group, Camp Abu Naji or British presence in Al Amarah. The following day as the Merlin helicopter grunted and strained to lift the mines back to Basra for demolition, I reflected that operational tours are packed with surreal moments, and this had been one of them.

The following day I returned to the PJOC to discuss bomb disposal training for the Iraqis but instead found myself being ushered into a small office in the centre of which stood a rickety plastic table, a single chair and what looked a lot like eight improvised grenades and a military hand grenade, all neatly arranged in a row. Of varying sizes, I could see that the improvised grenades had been constructed from artillery exploders (part of an artillery shell) and cut down detonators, which made them very dangerous indeed. I looked at Rich, who shrugged his shoulders and smiled.

'You defuse!' The Iraqi Police Colonel pointed excitedly at his desk. 'You bomb engineer! You defuse!'

I looked at Rich, seeking support. This was crazy; eight grenades and I had few tools, no x-rays and no blast proof area within which to work. Rich knew these guys inside out and would be the right man to negotiate.

'You're the ATO – good luck!' Rich chuckled under his breath as he walked slowly backwards away from the bombs and out of the room. He closed the door gently as he left.

Taking stock, I wondered how I had got to be here, in the centre of an Iraqi town with nine bombs to defuse by hand. I took out a pair of forensic gloves from my webbing, laid out my tools to complete the task and inspected each grenade. I would never see eight simpler IEDs in my career but they were still potentially lethal. To defuse them I would have to remove the detonator that had been inserted into each exploder by hand. Detonators are made to initiate very easily; if I held them too tightly, dropped them or if there was too much friction between the detonator and exploder, it would initiate and I would lose my hands, my sight, and possibly my life.

No one ever described defusing bombs like this on my IED courses. I could handle the worst that Al Qaeda could throw at me but was now reliant on a healthy dose of luck to succeed. I slowly pulled the detonator out of the first grenade and put it to one side. The next was not so easy; a small burr of metal stopped me removing the detonator and I had to tug harder than I would have liked.

I nearly fainted when a loud bang echoed around the room.

Behind me the door had flown open. A young Iraqi policeman walked in, raised both eyebrows in acknowledgement, pointed nervously towards the solitary wooden chair in the room, picked it up, gave me a thumbs up and smiled encouragingly as he left. I nodded politely before completing my task, laughing to myself as I worked. Finally, after years of hard work, I was here, doing exactly what I wanted.

I was making a difference.

4. AL KHALA

22 December 2005

A single lamp burned away inside the two-storey house, its faint glow, barely visible through the ground floor windows, the only sign of life on this pitch black night.

Our target, Abu Omar Al-Husseini, known to us as Bravo 546, and his wife, Bravo 582, were responsible for arming many of the militias that fought us and each other for control of Al Amarah.

I had never been to this house before but knew it intimately. The hours spent poring over maps, aerial photographs and witness reports ensured that, before we got anywhere near the town, I knew the layout of each room, who would be asleep in each bed and where 546 stored his arsenal. Most of all, I knew that this house belonged to the biggest arms dealer in southern Iraq and that he worked from home. I expected to find 107mm rockets, RPGs, AK-47s and RPK machine guns, enough for a small army.

But that was nothing. We knew that he had just received a shipment of Surface to Air Missiles (SAMs) and satellite images had shown recent digging in the compound that surrounded the house. One SAM could bring down a Hercules C-130 with sixty troops on board; this was the most important arrest operation Al Amarah had ever seen.

Al-Husseini was almost mythical in Al Amarah. Less than

a month ago we didn't even know whether he actually existed.
I knew everything about his operation but had never seen a
photo or heard a description of him. I had, however, heard the
crack of his lethal wares as they zipped over my head in town
far too many times. He was the worst kind of criminal: he really
didn't care who he sold weapons to, wasn't political and backed
whoever had the money to keep him happy. At least the terrorists believed in something more than cash.

The clock would start ticking as soon as this arrest went
noisy: it would take the hooligans from Al Mak about 30
minutes to hear of our raid, mount up and dart up Route 6 to
take us on. It would be full-scale war if they got to us earlier
than expected. The Battle Group wanted to get in, do the job
and then get the hell out of there before Maysaan province
disintegrated into mayhem.

I would have been happy to wait 35 minutes; no one had been
punished for the deaths of the Red Caps – the six military
policemen killed by an Iraqi mob in 2003 – and it would be the
same guys charging towards us as soon as we smashed our way
into this house. I would sooner have had a JDAM dropped
from 18,000 feet and keep the Battle Group out of harm's way,
but there was absolutely no political will for that. I just had to
hope they would be quicker than we thought.

At least 50 metres from its nearest neighbour, the house was
conspicuous in its opulence as it stood imposingly amongst the
single-storey shacks that made up the rest of Al Khala. A tall,
white, brick wall surrounded the house, only the gaps in the
two formidable iron gates at the front and rear allowing any
view of the building.

Peering through gaps in the front gate I could see the front
door to the house flanked by small windows on either side, with
three concrete steps leading up to it only 10 metres away. Less
than a metre in front of me the front gate was locked by a solitary

65

metal slide, held in place by a flimsy padlock. In contrast, the rear gate was securely locked from the inside with two thick grey padlocks connecting heavy wrought-iron chains which had rusted from neglect and lack of use. Snaking around the right-hand side of the building were steps which ran up the side of the house directly to the roof which was surrounded by a white wall about half a metre high.

I could also see that the compound comprised a barren mix of grass and earth. In the south-east corner of the compound the earth had been dug up and replaced within the last week and deep tyre tracks led away from the disturbed earth, through my position and into the distance behind me. The intelligence was spot on – something had been dug in within the last few days.

The tracks had filled with rainwater overnight and my boots were caked in mud; around me I could see others in a similar position. Only minutes before we had tried to glide silently into position but had squelched and cursed as we patrolled the couple of kilometres from the holding area where our vehicles remained out of sight. Only the sound of the rain drumming loudly on to nearby roofs had masked our approach.

As soon as my watch showed 0330 hours this quiet neigh-bourhood was going to erupt with shouts, lights and gunfire. It was now 0328. The dim lights which lit the house looked almost inviting, with the white walls of the building giving it a Mediterranean look. To my left and right I could hear the laboured breathing of the men with whom I had just tabbed to this area. Only 2 kilometres behind us the Warriors, my EOD van and our Quick Reaction Force waited in the holding area, a large forest made up of irregularly spaced palm trees that had often served as a launch point for the rocket attacks on our camp, but which now concealed two companies of armoured infantrymen champing at the bit, ready to sprint towards us when it went noisy.

The silence was broken by the buzz of the PRR.

'One minute.'

The OC, Major Caller, was at the very back of our group and had coordinated our raid with Merlin helicopters carrying medics and a Sea King with an infrared camera mounted underneath. Known as 'Heli Telly', it would film the entire op and keep an eye out for terrorist reinforcements arriving from Al Amarah or Al Mak. I strained to hear them but could not; they would be hovering in the pitch black, a couple of kilometres but only a matter of seconds away so as not to alert the Bravos of the impending operation.

'30 seconds.' I felt queasy as the words of SAT, the EOD Group's in-house IEDD expert, John Hall, rattled in my ears.

'If there's any fucking shooting stay low – and remember these fuckers would rather detonate themselves than get arrested.'

He was right; I had seen videos of other arrest ops where the terrorists had blown themselves up seconds before they would have been captured. If we did get a suicide bomber it would be up to me to disarm him.

'10 seconds.'

My heart seemed ready to burst through my ribcage as my stomach grew yet queasier. I moved back, around the corner of the compound wall, out of sight of the front gates and covered my ears. I felt like a sprinter in the blocks, ready to explode into action. My muscles tensed as I mentally counted down the last few seconds. This was going to be loud.

'3 ... 2 ... 1 ... GO GO GO!' By the second 'Go' the front gates to the compound had been blown off their hinges, we had felt the blast wave pass through us and the night for a fraction of a second became bright daylight. The clock had begun. Thirty minutes to go.

Large lumps of what used to be a padlock flew through the air away from the house as I sprinted through the still swinging gates. The weight of my body armour, tools and rifle was forgotten as I ran towards the house. Ahead of me the assault team had already smashed the front door with a thick metal battering ram and I could hear them shouting at the occupants in pidgin Arabic to stay still. Behind me, Corporal Sniper, the engineer search team commander, was already screaming orders at his team.

'Jonesy and Jonno rip those fucking tarps off those mounds, NOW. Simmo, get inside that fucking shed and give it the once over, NOW. Stevie get inside that fucking house and tear it apart . . . everybody got it? NOW!'

If there was a single round of ammunition here, these guys would find it.

The net was alive with updates as the assault teams moved from room to room on the ground floor, the torches fixed to their SA8os flashing around in the dust like light sabres as four-man teams cleared each room. Doors were smashed in by the first member, warnings shouted by the second and third as they entered the room and the rear covered by the fourth man. They had only a few seconds in each room, time to search for anyone hiding or worse still – ready to fight.

'Ground floor clear – no Bravos.'

They had found no one downstairs but the three teams springing up the stairs hoped to have more success in the bedrooms on the first floor. I went with them; Iraqi terrorists tend to keep anything illegal as close to them as possible. I had found a loaded RPG under the terrorist's bed on the last strike op, with crates of 12.7mm ammunition stored in the children's wardrobes. Outside, the Iraqi police had been tasked with clearing the roof, a straightforward task that would involve them without placing the success of operation in jeopardy. They were keen to succeed and impress the Brits but were poorly trained and possessed mainly outdated equipment. Hopefully they would get to the roof, find nothing and stay safe.

'Roger – we've got Bravo 546.' As I stood at the top of the stairs I saw a figure in a long white gown being led from the main bedroom and towards me. This couldn't be him; he looked far too old, too frail – just too normal. This man was at least 60 and looked as if he could barely climb out of bed, let alone run a weapons-smuggling business. Behind him a woman was shouting loudly and slapping away the hands of the two huge Highlanders that had been assigned to arrest her. Bravo 582 was putting up much more of a fight than her husband.

Looking around I could see walls covered in photographs, family portraits hanging next to images of children, and ornaments standing on every surface, just like every house I had been into in Londonderry, Strabane and Portrush. It was neater than my room in the mess in Germany. Just as in Londonderry, this was a family home. How could someone with children be responsible for so much death?

'ATO.' The infantry search commander waved me towards the smaller bedroom.

'Take a look at all this shit.' He gestured inside the room; the solid wooden wardrobes which stood on the right-hand side of the room had been opened and clothing dragged out on to the floor. At the bottom of each wardrobe sat an array of weaponry, shiny and new, straight from the factory.

No one had touched a thing – once they found the hardware I took over. There were too many opportunities for cock-ups, weapons still to be loaded and sensitive explosive materials to cause these guys harm. I moved to the furthest open door and looked inside. In a second I saw an RPK machine gun, and three RPG warheads. Bingo.

'Fucking brilliant! Well done boys. Get on the net and tell the ...'

'GRENADE!' As the searcher next to me had picked up a pile of clothes a hand grenade had dropped from the bundle, thudded against the floor and was now rolling towards me.

The room went deadly silent.

I had nowhere to go, nothing to duck under and could only spectate as the dull green egg-shaped grenade rumbled toward me in slow motion. The distinctive long aluminium fuse sticking out from the top was instantly recognizable; the RGD-5 grenade was Russian made, notoriously unreliable, and had a delay that ranged from 0–13 seconds. Right now only one thing mattered – where was the pin?

Five sets of eyes bored into the grenade as it rolled lazily in my direction. It came to a halt as it circled and struck the bottom of the wardrobe. The pin was in.

'Fucking Hell! ... for fuck's sake!' I shouted at nobody, just needing the release of tension. I still couldn't take my eyes off the grenade.

Any fear I had felt was nothing compared to the horror that was written all over the searcher's face. He was as white as a sheet and as conversation slowly returned to the room I even felt sorry for him – Corporal Sniper would tear him apart.

There was no time to reflect. By now the Mahdi army would be sending some of their brightest and best from Al Majar Al Kabir, a fleet of pickup trucks would be heading our way, bristling with DShk machine guns and RPG-7s.

I quickly unscrewed the fuse from the RGD-5 and carefully searched around each weapon before dragging it from its hiding place. I knew better than to make assumptions about terrorists and it would definitely be an assumption too far to guess that they wouldn't booby-trap something in their own house. Even if they were not that crazy I had to be careful; a single detonator dropped, mistreated or struck could initiate the C-4 explosive that had been squashed into every corner of the wardrobe.

As each item was made safe, I passed it to Claire who bagged and tagged it. She had set up a ferociously efficient conveyor belt and dragged tough infantrymen into writing details of weapons, photographing every item and placing them all in transparent forensic bags. Tough guys, experienced soldiers and hard nuts from all corners of Scotland were coerced into action as she barked instructions and corrected mistakes.

As I worked, the searchers dragged out drawers, lifted mattresses and kept striking gold. An RPG launcher appeared from underneath the bed, then long belts of 7.62mm ammunition, then more OG-7 anti-personnel rounds appeared from this Aladdin's cave. They hadn't even bothered to hide it; all of our loot lay under the bed surrounded by shoes, socks and long-forgotten rubbish. Even the Bogside wasn't quite *this* bad.

Had that old man on the stairs, who rubbed sleep from his eyes as he walked downstairs, really been the kingpin of the most significant gun-running operation in the area? He had children, whose room I was now in but whom I had yet to see, and his house seemed well ordered, familial and, well, *normal.*

He would say that he was a businessman; I thought he was as bad as the guys pulling the trigger. It was well known that many of the terrorists in Iraq only fought the coalition for money. There were going rates for shooting a soldier, planting a bomb or taking out a tank. It was possible to make a healthy living just by planting the occasional roadside bomb, filming the results for proof and collecting the cash from the local Al Qaeda or Mahdi army leader. It depressed me beyond belief that I had probably been shot at many times by people who saw me not as a soldier but as a pay cheque.

Room clear. The main bedroom was even better – boxes of Fl grenades, a brand new PKM machine gun and a wardrobe full of the ubiquitous AKs. Rich Holmes had found thousands of US dollars in a drawer and was now carefully labelling a clear plastic bag with his find. There was enough ammo in here to keep the streets of Al Amarah flowing with blood for at least another month.

Outside in the compound the REST had no luck. These guys were the best searchers in the world but they had found nothing. The outbuilding was empty apart from stacks of old bricks, the tarpaulin covered huge piles of sand and there was no sign of the SAMs anywhere.

I had my first glimpse of the children, a boy and girl both aged about 12, as I walked back into the house to collect my kit and saw the family lined up behind the weapons which covered the floor of the entrance corridor. A photographer recorded the events for the Iraqi courts. It was very simple. If you could produce a photo of a man with a gun he would go to jail. The children stood next to their parents, wide-eyed and nervous. The young girl's small hand grasped her father's sleeve as the flash lit the room; the boy stood perfectly still and looked terrified.

We had just taken a serious amount of military equipment off the streets, undoubtedly saving lives – and yet I felt little happiness. Not only had we missed out on the rockets and SAMs, but I was seeing a family torn apart before my eyes. Al-Husseini was bad, and I hated him for putting profit before life, but as I looked at them standing there I wondered whether the children deserved to have their parents locked up for years to come.

'Shit, isn't it.' Rich Holmes approached from the opposite direction and nodded towards the scene as the flash once again lit up the room.

'Word is they were tipped off about our visit and moved the rockets late last night. They thought we wouldn't give a damn about the rifles and RPGs and never even bothered to move them.' He paused as we looked at the family. Al-Husseini looked back and smiled.

'And don't worry about the kids either. He'll be out before this reaches the courts; a couple of bribes and he will just slip away. Anyway, come up to the roof – you need to see this.'

The eight Iraqi policemen stood proudly around their loot as we reached the top of the steps. In the middle of the roof, mortar bombs, small arms ammunition and a grenade had been scattered around. Rich gave them a big thumbs up, smiled and muttered under his breath.

'They dropped all this stuff here.' I raised an eyebrow as we turned and walked back to the front gate of the compound.

'It was these guys who tipped off Al-Husseini. They thought he would shift all the gear but wanted to look good in our eyes so brought a bag of tricks with them. Heli telly caught it all on camera; they ran up the steps, emptied the bag on the ground and then stood around waiting for applause.'

I tried to laugh, but could only shake my head.

'So the Iraqi Police tipped off a guy who in any case will bribe his way out of jail and then planted a load of shit just to make themselves look good? Thank fuck we've at least taken the weapons off the street.' I sighed and slowly rubbed my forehead; Rich looked at me and smiled. Then it clicked. I was so naive.

'We weren't here to get any weapons were we? We were here so the politicians could say that we were working with the Iraqi Police – that all was well in Al Amarah.' Rich shrugged his shoulders and laughed.

'Who fucking knows. The point is that those weapons,' he gestured towards the arsenal which now covered most of the floor, 'aren't going to hurt you, me or anyone else in Al Amarah.

And even if this war is fucked up, that's got to be a good thing, right?!'

At least the generals and politicians would be happy; another show of joint UK and Iraqi operations apparently succeeding. It seemed to me that this success had been superficial at best.

The OC appeared at the stairs and tapped his watch.

'Right, let's get going. Our buddies from Al Mak are on Route 6 and we need to get out of here before they arrive.'

Behind him I could see the Warriors, which had arrived shortly after the assault, revving their engines. They had begun to sink into the thick mud and fared little better than their crew, who increasingly struggled against the suction of the earth as their feet were enveloped by mud.

My EOD van had no armour to speak of, little protection from bullets, bombs or RPGs but was totally resistant to bullshit and the intellectual vacuum that existed within the UK's 'strategy' in Iraq. In here I could relax, unwind and escape from the web of politics that UK forces had spun for themselves. If we weren't interested in actually achieving anything in Al Amarah why on earth were we here? This op was the military equivalent of fast food; it looked great and tasted even better but was utterly pointless.

As the tyres spun in the mud before jolting us forward, I looked at my watch; it was 0356 hours.

The Battle Group had scored a victory over the militias in Al Amarah and strangled their supply of weaponry for a short time. More would soon arrive from Iran to take its place, but right now, for a few days at least, the flow had stopped and we had made a difference.

Every weapon taken off the street was one less to fire aimed shots at us and indiscriminate shots at those Iraqis keen to pursue peace and go about their normal lives. Back in camp, I laid our haul out at the back of EOD House in preparation for it to be shipped to Basra and eventually to the UK. We could recover vital forensic evidence, establish where the weapons had come from and make plans to smash weapon supply routes.

I had felt odd about the arrest after seeing Al-Husseini with his children, but now the pity had disappeared. Fuck him, I thought. If he wants to make a living supplying terrorists then he had to deal with the consequences. I struggled to shake the image of his children stood in their own living room looking at their father, handcuffed and with a British hand on his collar, but put it to the back of my mind.

Claire had done an incredible job in cataloguing the weapons at the scene but now as she appeared from the EOD Ops room she had a face like thunder.

'What a waste of fucking time.' She began to pick up the carefully arranged rifles and throw them into a pile.

'What do you mean? What are you doing?' Now *I* was pissed off.

'We have to give them all back to the Iraqi police tomorrow and they will just sell them to whoever the fuck has enough cash. I am so sick of this place.'

After all that effort, the risk of the assault and of being ambushed on our way back by the Mahdi army, the general in Basra had decided that as a show of goodwill we should turn over the weapons to the Iraqi police. They had, after all, done an *excellent* job themselves during the arrest.

I exhaled loudly and sat down on the pile of wooden pallets outside my explosives store. What a waste. No forensics, no ballistics, and now we had every chance of seeing these weapons in the hands of people whose sole aim was to kill British soldiers. I didn't sit down for long and my blood boiled as I stomped around.

'Six fucking Red Caps get slaughtered in Al Mak, what do

we do? Fuck all. We get fucking rocketed every night and what do we do? Fuck all. How the fuck will we ever win this war if our own side won't let us take the fight to these people?'

I looked at Claire and shrugged my shoulders. There was little we could do, except perhaps search another old man's house and find the same weapons once again.

That night Martin the Padre had organized an officers' DVD night, a chance for us all to unwind and, just as importantly, give our soldiers the chance to do the same. The DVDs were generally designed to relax, to give us opportunity to reflect and escape from the reality of Iraq for a couple of hours. It was also a chance for the officers of the Battle Group to meet in much less formal surroundings; the CO would sit on the floor at the front whilst others occupied benches and chairs behind him. I had sometimes found it so relaxing to slump in the cotton chairs that I had nodded off, only to be awoken by the howls of laughter during the film.

Tonight *Four Weddings and a Funeral* played on the makeshift screen, which had been fashioned from a white sheet hanging from the roof of the small chapel which for tonight only had been commandeered by the Officers' Mess. The smell of the incense that burned constantly in the corner of the chapel filled the room but I could not rest. The thought of handing over these weapons made me fume with anger and I was determined to do something about it. All the serial numbers had been logged so there was no way I could just throw them away or hide them. Halfway through the film I got up, left and ran back to EOD House, grabbing Claire from the office where she was finishing her report on the find.

'Fuck this, they can have the guns but not before I have finished with them.' She followed me to the locked ISO container and duly opened the padlock. Over the next hour I dismantled each weapon, removed all the gas parts, firing pins and breech blocks and threw them in the store. The RPGs were next; the rocket motors were made of sticks of propellant which fell out after I sliced through the cardboard cover holding them in place. You cannot fire the RPG without its rocket motor and I wasn't ready to hand over lethal anti-armour weapons to anybody, including the Iraqi police.

The next morning I handed my cargo of unusable weaponry to the Para section that had been tasked with delivering it to town. They were even more pissed off than we were at returning the weapons and had the same thought as me, albeit without the subtlety: a stray Warrior was found to crush the machine guns before handing them back.

Day after day the Battle Group was pulverized by rockets and pounded by small-arms fire and yet, for the sake of politics, we were ordered to hand back weapons to the Iraqi police. I may as well have loaded the rifles and sprayed the camp with 7.62mm rounds myself.

5. IN THE RED

22 February 2006

With only three weeks of my tour remaining I was looking forward to Charlie Yorke, my friend and replacement, arriving in two weeks time and to me getting out of Iraq. I had enjoyed my time here, but was worn down by the constant need to be ready at a moment's notice, the fear experienced on tasks such as the culvert, and the endless rocket barrages which had left the Battle Group mentally exhausted.

Rocket attacks were signalled by the camp alarm system wailing around 10 seconds after the dull crump of distant explosion. Occasionally it was possible to hear the loud whoooosh of a rocket being launched, and then, some 20–30 seconds later, an almighty thud as it impacted around us.

So far during my tour, fifty rockets had been launched at Camp Abu Naji. Thankfully they had not killed anyone, but their far more subtle and increasingly widespread effect was slowly grinding away our will to fight.

The wailing alarms and quake-like explosions were nothing compared to the high-pitched screech as rockets accelerated towards the earth. This hellish scream from the sky was a fraction of a second long but seemed, in our minds, to last a lifetime. Every time the earth shook under the bombardments, whenever the night was briefly turned into day by the fluorescence of high explosive, our reserves of courage were chipped

Amarah, fighting and war disappeared and were replaced by laughter as tales of the day's fuck-ups were relayed to anyone within earshot.

Crump.

The windows shook slightly.

At first nothing happened, no one moved. The sound could have been anything. Near the fridges, chefs raised both hands and shook their heads (days earlier a sous chef had nearly been lynched after slamming a door and terrifying the entire Battle Group). Eyes met across the canteen and ears tuned into the bass frequency of high explosive. We were in the blocks, ready to be launched, but no one was sure whether the starter's pistol had just fired. Slowly, stares disengaged and forks were moved back towards plates. Nervous chatter began to break out amongst those keenest to show that they were not worried.

Crump.

The whole canteen shook.

Within a second eyes had met again, invisible acknowledgements exchanged and all hell broke loose. Men fought each other for body armour and combat helmets, friends jostled for position under tables and eyes that minutes earlier had been filled only with laughter were once again filled with fear.

The floor was soon littered with plastic chairs as these were kicked out from underneath tables to make room for more people. It was selfish and ugly – human survival instinct at its most basic. The Scots DGs was a Battle Group at the peak of its fighting powers but now we were fixed in position by rockets that could be bought in the border towns for less than $20 each. Hundreds of millions of pounds of armour and sophisticated communications and weaponry sat idle as its operators cowered under thin tables that would in any case offer no protection from supersonic fragmentation.

The last explosion had been close, much closer than the first, and we knew there would be more to come. Every person in the Battle Group had seen photos of improvised rocket launchers and had seen on insurgent videos the largest of them all, one with eight tubes, launching death into the night. If we were lucky, they would only fire a few.

Crump.

Even closer, near the med centre. The alarm wailed incessantly in the background, telling us that we were under attack and the terrorists that they were on target. Each person mentally counted off each rocket as it detonated. Three so far, that could be it. Or there could be five left.

I left the sea of swarming bodies behind as I dashed for the exit. Right now, Battle Group Ops would be in frenzied activity locating the launch site and receiving casualty reports from around the camp. They wouldn't go near a firing point without me. There was no choice; I had to run.

A young paratrooper stood in my way as I ran toward the door.

'Sorry Sir, no one is allowed out. CO's orders, it's safer in here.'

'What?' I was incredulous.

'You're not allowed out during rocket attacks.'

'Of course I am – *I'm ATO!*' I looked at the poor paratrooper who stood in my way and implored him to move. Moments after he moved aside I burst out of the door and immediately chastised myself for sounding like such a prize dick. Had I really said, 'Of course I am, *I'm ATO*'? I hadn't calmly explained that my place was in the Ops room and that the risk was worth it – I had emphasised '*I'm ATO*' as if it was my divine right to risk my life for no good reason whatsoever. Before the words had left my mouth I realized what a pompous, arrogant idiot I must have sounded.

I was still shaking my head as I crouched down outside the

canteen and fumbled with my torch. The smoke and smell of high explosive filled my nostrils as the door slammed behind me; I was very much on my own.

Crump. Fuck! I dropped the torch and scrabbled around on the floor with my hands outstretched. I was losing time and was even more vulnerable than the poor guys in the canteen. Fuck it. I left my torch and prepared to sprint over the open ground towards the Hesco Bastion fortress that protected the Ops room. With around 200 metres of open ground to cross and the siren still warning me of incoming rockets, I was in real danger. My body armour, tight around my chest, made my breathing much more laboured than usual. The combat helmet which so often sat at a jaunty angle on my head was readjusted, the chinstrap tightened and I took a deep breath.

Go.

Within a second of standing up, the high-pitched shriek of a 107mm Katyusha rocket pierced the night above me. It impacted outside the wire, some 30 metres to the west of camp, but close enough for the detonation wave to bully its way through the earth and up my legs. I hadn't made it more than 10 metres away from the canteen, was in no man's land and was frozen to the spot, absolutely terrified of moving in any direction. Fight or flight time. I could curl up beside the thick Hesco bastion that surrounded the canteen and be relatively safe – or do my job and get to the Ops room.

Go.

I sprinted over the hard-baked earth from the door of the canteen towards the tank park, 200 metres of open space in which I would be unprotected from the blast and iron shards that would soon be flying around at ten times the speed of sound. My heart pumped hard as I began to cover the ground; only 180 metres in front of me was safety. Distant explosions caused the night to light up for a hundredth of a second, simultaneously showing me my route and destroying any night vision that aided me in the dark.

150 metres to go and in the distance the 'whoooosh' of a rocket launch indicated that another was coming. The rocket travelled at 300 metres per second and would arrive by the time I had covered only another 30 metres. With the Ops room still impossibly far away, the agonizing scream of a rocket in terminal descent grew louder and seemed to be coming from all directions at once. My legs pounded the ground as adrenalin drove me forward, faster, more desperate than ever to survive this barrage.

To my left, the ground erupted as earth was cast into the air and the intense heat of the TNT detonating scorched the side of my face. Milliseconds after the explosion, dozens of other sounds, the 'whup, whup, whup' of razor-sharp metal cutting through the filthy air seemed to last for an eternity. The lazy bass sound of low-velocity fragments sounded like the slow-motion helicopter rotors in Vietnam films. It was as terrifying as the whistle that preceded each explosion – and far more deadly. These large lumps of the rocket casing would take a man's head off or rip his leg from him, and the air was filled with them.

'*I'm ATO*,' I whined aloud to myself. '*I'm ATO and I'm a stupid prick.*' If I was going to die during this tour, I hoped to God it wasn't after acting like such a tool.

Go!

My lungs burned and my legs felt like lead as I raced over the last 30 metres. As I rounded the corner of the barricade I saw Captain James Rogers, the Bravo Company 2IC completing a similar dash from his accommodation. We had made it, and exchanged grins as we stood with hands on hips, unable to speak. I stepped towards James, who by now was walking into the building, and motioned to let him through first as I still gasped for breath, when, to the east of camp, a huge explosion rocked the main gate.

Whup, whup, whup.

We had both heard this sound so many times. Agonizingly, we had enough time to understand what was happening but nowhere near enough to do anything about it. James' face transformed from a relieved smile to a look of absolute terror. I had seen that look only minutes earlier in the canteen after the first explosion and I now saw it close up. The bravest of men share with the most cowardly the expression of helpless fear, and for a fraction of a second become children; scared, lonely and utterly powerless. For a moment the sound grew louder as each of us stood rooted to the spot. It was up to luck now. We would die, or we wouldn't.

Whup, whup, whup.

The wall turned to dust as the rocket struck it. Only a metre from my head and 30 centimetres from James, a solid metal Katyusha rocket motor struck the Ops room and nearly penetrated the wall. There was no explosion, no heat, no detonation, but the air filled with dust and each of us knew just how close we had come to being killed.

Shocked faces met James and me as we burst into the Ops room. Looking at James, I could see why. He was coated in dust and sweat and stood hunched over with his hands on his knees, catching his breath. I could see the relief and exhaustion on his face from where I was standing, similarly hunched over, gasping for breath and spitting out dust.

'Ah good, ATO.' The Battle Group Battle Major breezed in through the door that James and I had almost taken off its hinges, and slurped loudly from his mug of tea.

'We have located the firing point. We've had twelve inbound so far and the possibility of more to come. Fast air has been over and seen a number of hot spots, some of which have moved away from the firing point.'

'So we have the rocket team?' Our next actions seemed so clear that I asked what I thought would be a rhetorical question. 'Is the Tornado going to take them out?'

His eyes looked tired. 'The RAF won't consider dropping any ordnance unless they catch them in the act, so as soon as they leave the firing point they are as free as a bird.'

'So . . .' He held up his hand before I could finish. 'So we just have to sit here and take it.' He had finished my sentence for me. I was furious.

'So what the fuck is the point of having them up there at all?' Sympathetic heads nodded in unison around the Ops room. In the past week the Battle Group had lost a man due to the sheer mental pressure of these attacks. These rockets were unsophisticated, cheap, inaccurate and in some cases decades old. But their attacks on our courage were laser-guided and he had seen enough. It wasn't just the rockets falling that had caused him to crack; it was the knowledge that they would never stop. He needed to be airlifted back to Basra with a shrink sitting next to him on the flight. Our casualties from bullets and bombs had been lighter than most Battle Groups, but the onslaught and lack of offensive action to combat the attacks had taken its toll on all of us.

Crump, Crump.

'That's fourteen, Sir.' The Royal Artillery detachment responsible for identifying and analysing launch sights and impact points had declared a new record. On their desk the small monitor displayed a map of Al Amarah. At the bottom left-hand corner, Camp Abu Naji was highlighted in green. To the north east, from one point by the river, fourteen separate red lines showed the flight path of each rocket and its impact. Eight had fallen within the camp, with the other six peppering the area outside. Incredibly, no one had been killed or physically injured, but each person in the Battle Group had their reserves of courage depleted once again. In this battle of slow mental attrition the enemy were winning.

Fourteen rockets hurt, but nowhere near as much as the attacks that followed the *News of the World* front page story that came out at the same time, on alleged British abuses in Al Amarah. Taken from video footage, the pictures seemed to show British soldiers in Al Amarah controlling a riot and dragging three young Iraqi men inside their base in the centre of town before assaulting them. Just a few days after the newspaper was published, I had once again dodged rockets as the biggest barrage of my tour turned areas of Camp Abu Naji into sheets of flying steel. I lost count of how many landed, but the next day the *Telegraph* reported that it had been as many as twenty. There were also a number of shootings in town and the Battle Group was lucky not to suffer more fatalities.

I hoped the *News of the World* had sold a few more copies, made a bit more money and felt it had done a good deed, because that night I returned to my room, held my head in my hands and shook with fear. For the first time I wondered whether I had it in me to complete this tour, whether I was too far in the red, whether there was any chance of ever seeing my family again.

The events that appeared to have taken place were unforgivable, totally against the ethos of the British Army and demanded investigation. But to fill the front page of a newspaper with those images instead of handing them to the police, put a gun to every man and woman's head in Camp Abu Naji. We wouldn't now get away with just a rocket attack and some shootings. That video energized the local militia, and everything the Battle Group had done to aid reconstruction was forgotten as the images replayed again and again on local television sets.

I could accept being under threat if it meant completing our mission and helping to reconstruct Iraq, but the thought of my friends being injured or killed so that an editor could claim the 'story of the year' made my blood boil.

As the end of February approached, the whole Battle Group was on edge. We had been lucky so far, but we all knew that casualties were not too far away and that there was worse to come. I had seen some action during my tour and had been lucky enough to have had relatively few successful IED attacks in my area. There had been no 'horror task' where I had been tested to my limits, but the mental result was the same; the cumulative effect of so many attacks and tasks on the streets had left me with little courage.

Days previously, I had noticed my hands shaking uncontrollably whilst trying to eat. As I tried to disguise my nerves I looked around and saw that I was not the only one.

It was definitely time to go home.

6. JUST ANOTHER DAY

28 February 2006

Sweat poured from the exhausted forehead of the lead scout as he inched forward, his progress in the 45° heat agonizingly slow. The lives of the seven men behind him, his friends, depended solely on him holding his nerve, remembering his drills and simply being lucky.

The patrol had already travelled 40 metres down the track to get to this point, changing point man every 10 metres. It was Corporal Stevie Jack's turn to take the risk now, with the remainder of the patrol positioned well behind him. There was no point fragging everyone. The lucky few had tucked themselves behind rocks; others lay prone, in full view of the kill zone but with nowhere else to go. All eyes burned into Stevie's back. They all knew exactly how he felt, each of them having spent enough time wrestling with their own fears to know that all they could do was shut up, keep their eyes peeled for the enemy and hope to God that nothing happened.

The intelligence had been very clear: a claymore IED had been planted along this route late last night. Only last week an entire patrol had been cut to ribbons by the same kind of bomb. They knew it was here somewhere, but amidst all the rubble, garbage and the crap that gathered in every Iraqi gutter, Stevie was more likely to find it as he was thrown through the air than through his steamed-up SUSAT sight.

The gravel track wound around a few single-storey buildings for another 30 metres before joining the tarmac road. A knee-high sand berm packed with litter and old cans and covered in discarded wrappers followed the right-hand edge of the track, piled on top of light grey kerbstones that had been torn apart by Warrior tracks.

Forget a claymore – you could hide a battalion's worth of C4 plastic explosive in there and never see it.

An old Coke bottle jutted out conspicuously from the high point of the berm, its mouth jammed into the yellow sand. A foot down from the bottle the sand had been recently disturbed and was now moist and dark, in stark contrast to the rest of the berm.

To the left of the track, sparse trees provided perfect aiming markers for distant assailants with their fingers hovering over radio switches. From the tree closest to him an old grey sock hung, swaying in the wind; only a few metres further on, white tape had been wrapped around the thin trunk of a palm tree.

Shit.

Stevie had no idea that only 2 metres in front of him the claymore was primed and aimed directly at his front. He would be blown to pieces and never know what had hit him. Behind him, his mates would be shredded in a thousandth of a second, the lucky ones dying instantly, the others seeing themselves bleed out on to the filthy Iraqi streets before closing their eyes.

The PIR, hidden inside a kerbstone, was infinitely patient and never failed. These guys, Highlanders, had been through this road a dozen times before and were good, but not this good. They had no chance; there was no way they would spot it; the only sign, a small black plastic disc covering the PIR, was barely visible through the yellow grime that coated everything in Iraq.

Only 50cm away – he still hadn't seen it.

His left boot hovered a further 10cm forward. As he lowered first his toes and then his heel the solid crunch of gravel was heaven, a sure sign that it really was road, not a pressure mat that was taking his weight. His right boot slid into place seconds later. Relief, time to breathe, then start again. SUSAT up, scan the area ahead, look again with the Mark One Eyeball, hold your breath and inch forward another despairingly small distance.

They had been on the road for an hour and seen nothing. Maybe the intelligence was crap? He knew this road as well as anyone, had been up and down it at least once a week since arriving in theatre and could see nothing out of place. Yet.

Just 30cm away – he stopped, crouched and slowly scanned the area to his front, left to right, right to left, painfully deliberate, for a few minutes the bravest man in the world.

He's missed it – he's getting up – in a few seconds the PIR will see him and it will be all over. His leg drifted toward the PIR's field of view and then stopped suddenly.

He spins towards me, a huge smile spreading across his face.

'No fucking chance, ATO! I seen it five minutes ago!' He pointed at the small plastic disc as his patrol threw off their helmets and laughed aloud. 'You have to be better than that ATO – this is Charlie Three Alpha, the best fucking soldiers in Eye – Fucking – Rack!' I was delighted, they *were* good enough!

'You've made my day, boys!' I leapt from the Thinking Bomb and strode towards them. 'I don't care what anyone else in this Battle Group says ... you guys are alright! Now get some water in you before we try the next lane – and I'll get you fuckers there instead!'

That morning I had pushed beans around my plate as I reflected silently on the day to come. With only two weeks to push I was delighted and relieved at the thought of a day spent training, planning future strike operations and getting my team's equipment up to scratch in time for my handover to Charlie Yorke, now only 10 days away.

We had been due to go to the PJOC that day to recover some IED components the Iraqi Police had collected, but had been gazumped by a *Panorama* TV crew from the BBC. Over my orange juice I could see the journalists with the Parachute Regiment team that would take them into town. A few months ago I would have been furious at missing out on a trip into Al Amarah, but not now. I had barely slept the night before as innocuous sounds made me leap from bed and reach for my PRR at least half a dozen times. My hands were now shaking so badly that I was struggling to keep them on the right keys as I typed my IED reports.

I felt privileged to train the troops and relished the responsibility of doing so; an hour's training often stretched to fill an entire morning as keen infantrymen repeated their drills time and again. Early in the tour I could catch them out every time, but not now; they were superb and loved to let me know it. I would spend all day and all night helping them if they needed; if I spent every day outside the wire, I would want as much help as possible, too.

They had beaten me today, but I had other tricks up my sleeve and let them know it.

'Next time boys, you wait and see, you might be good but you are no Charlie Three Bravo. Now those boys were shit hot.'

I loved the banter during training. Whatever their background, soldiers could always find something to take the piss out of each other for. I had found their weak point: Charlie Three Bravo were another section in their platoon and any accusation of inferiority was like a kick to their balls. I had won again.

The laughter ebbed away as an ambulance screeched from the Battle Group Ops room towards our group. Within a few seconds it had careered around the crossroads outside EOD House and headed straight towards the Med Centre.

Our doctor, Lieutenant Commander Rick Andrews, ran from the Med Centre towards the ambulance. I could see the concentration on his face as he slung a large red object into the back and took his place in the commander's seat. It was bad news – that object was his trauma bergan, packed with life-saving medical equipment. This bergan had been used all too often in recent times. Rick had had a busy tour and was at the sharp end of the action more often than most of us, regularly performing miracles. Some people join the military because they have little other choice. Rick, with every choice in the world, was here with us.

Seconds later, on the tank park south of EOD House, plumes of black exhaust fumes spewed out from three Warriors as commanders climbing into the turret barked instructions to men diving through the rear door. Others threw shoebox-sized brown containers full of 7.62mm link and grenades from the back of Landrovers to the gunners who also appeared from the turret.

We stood silently, mere observers, as the Warriors powered toward the front gate. As exhausted and nervous as I was, there was little worse than the impotence of inaction – someone had been hurt and we were doing nothing. Any hint of an IED and I would mobilize my team and be ready in the Ops room before Battle Group Ops had even thought of contacting me.

We watched as the ambulance disappeared into the distance, shielding our drinks from the thick cloud of dust that its screeching tyres threw into the air and which now drifted over us. I imagined the troops in the back of the Warrior as it stormed out of camp, sweating in the intense heat, checking their rifles and pouring water down their necks. Everyone had their own way of preparing for a fight. Some sat silently, staring dead ahead; one or two would shake with fear, a few said a quiet prayer and others shouted at no one in particular: 'Come on boys – lets fucking do it. This is fucking it. Come on, fucking COME ON!'

The EOD House door crashed open as Jay burst out on to the road.

'Sir,' he was out of breath, 'It's the Battle Group Ops room and they need you now.'

I was on tunnel vision as I ran to the telephone. No other sounds, thoughts or distractions. Just get to the phone.

It was these moments that all soldiers lived for, and also those that they dreaded the most. With adrenalin pumping it is difficult not to feel invincible, but as a bomb disposal operator that is a very dangerous state of mind; complacency could kill me.

Jay held the door open as I sprinted past him to the EOD Ops room.

I picked up the phone. The familiar voice of JJ, an old friend of mine from college. His desk was right in the centre of the action, the Ops room, the beating heart of any Battle Group.

This could only be bad news.

'Contact IED – two fatalities, one secondary.' I could barely take it in as he continued: 'Not many details, but it happened around Red One in the centre of town.'

I looked at the spot map glued to the wall and traced the red route with my finger, stopping at the circle marked One. I knew the area well: this was the hardest part of Al Amarah. The red route was a long dual carriageway leading east-west, with the Olympic Stadium due south and large tracts of open, filthy ground to the north. High blocks of flats lining the route provided refuge for nests of snipers and formed a perfect vantage point for bombers. Red One was near to the main road junction in the centre of town where the patrol would have had to slow down, making them easier prey. The bombers were smart. They had chosen the ideal point for blowing up a patrol and following up with shootings and other bombs to target responders.

'Roger, I'll be at the Ops room in minutes few.' The handset swung from the table as I dashed back outside. Jay had already gathered the team together by the EOD van. 'This is it. This is the one. Let's go.'

Well-rehearsed drills fell into place as they sprang into action: Claire pulled webbing off hooks, Fitzy grabbed rifles and they all checked each other's kit.

My mind raced. JJ had said enough. I knew exactly what he meant: a bomb had functioned, killing two of our guys. I had no idea who the casualties were, where it had happened or what had caused it. For all I knew there could be twenty more casualties. Rick Andrews must have received the call a few minutes earlier.

I immediately began to wonder who had died. Did I know anyone out there today? What about my friend Danni, the Battle Group logistics officer? I was sure she'd be inside camp. Or Rhiannon, another doctor who I had often spent time with? She'd be fine, too; I'd seen her less than thirty minutes ago. There was something else, something I had missed:

'. . . one secondary.'

I started to shake. There was another bomb still out there. My bomb. A secondary device was normally designed to kill follow-up troops, the guys sent to the scene immediately to help, people like the QRF, the doctor. Me. I had just seen the QRF crashing towards town. Their dust still obscured the sun and the smell of diesel fumes hung in the air.

I had spent my life planning for this moment. I knew that the next few hours were exactly what I had been working towards; every single step had led me to Al Amarah and this task.

'There have been explosions in town near the Olympic Stadium. Two of the guys are dead and there's a secondary device.' Concentrated faces nodded back. They were scared, too. All of us were high on adrenaline and it showed: voices got louder, energy flowed around our bodies and any feelings of fatigue or tiredness were forgotten. 'Get ready! This is it, this is it ... get your kit together and meet me at the Battle Group Ops room.'

Sergeant Reynolds, the Royal Engineers Search Advisor (RESA) had only just returned from the gym and knew nothing of what had happened in the city. His transformation from healthy red to ashen faced was almost instantaneous. I would need him and his team to search for any hidden command wires – without them I would be going in blind. But he didn't know where his team were.

I felt sick.

'If you're not at Battle Group Ops in time, I'll leave without you. See you there.' He did not look confident as I ran out of the house and jumped into the EOD van alongside Fitzy, who was already wearing his combat helmet, webbing and PRR.

By leaving them behind I would be taking a much greater personal risk; without them I had no guarantee that the area was clear of command wires or secondary devices. But if waiting for them increased the amount of time, by a single second, that the infantry spent getting shot at, petrol bombed and potentially blown up, I'd have to leave them behind.

Battle Group Ops was a blur of activity. At the far end a huge map of Al Amarah covered an entire wall and was littered with hand-drawn symbols indicating the position of our troops in town. Large smudges indicated that a lot of troops were moving quickly around the battlespace and it was difficult to keep up.

Below the map, soldiers manning the huge bank of radios

screwed to the wall clutched their green handsets and made reams of notes, recording details and information from the ground as the CO and 2IC crouched over maps demanding more updates.

In the centre of the room was a single desk occupied by the Ops Officer, Captain Dillon Wilkins. It was Dillon who orchestrated our effort and whose role it was to coordinate the vast array of troops who were all speeding towards the scene, preparing to go or already returning with casualties. He was in full flow when I arrived, the Ops room moving to his tempo:

'Where is QRF 1?'

'En route to the scene sir, passing Sparrowhawk.' A young signaller pulled away from his handset to respond and then returned to the static which buzzed from his radio.

'Send QRF 2 out with the RSM – they will leave in five minutes. Get the ARF [airborne reaction force] on standby, I need them to pick up the bodies – wait out for timings.'

'Aye, sir.'

'And for fuck's sake tell the guys on the ground that we are sending troops to them now – they need to know help is on the way.'

With over a thousand moving parts speeding in different directions, and vast amounts of information pouring in from myriad sources, Dillon was immersed in the battle despite being 7 kilometres away from the action.

Organized chaos appeared to reign in those early minutes. No one knew enough. Decisions were being made everywhere and not always being coordinated, not always in the most effective way but always focused upon the main effort – getting our friends and colleagues out of danger and back to camp.

Information is the lifeblood of military operations and there is never enough of it. Battle Group Ops was under pressure from Brigade ops who were receiving demands from Divisional ops. The guys on the ground would suffer most – they provide all the information whilst fighting for their lives and looking after the dead and wounded. The inexperienced and most experienced are the quietest – either in shock or conscious of the value of calm when under pressure.

I grabbed Dillon by the shoulder and before he could respond had already asked him when I was going, who was I going with and if we knew any more about the bomb or the casualties. He knew nothing more than I had already heard; I was going in blind.

Dillon explained that QRF 1 had already left camp and were hurtling through Sparrowhawk airfield before arcing east on to the Red Route. They were closing in on the scene of the explosion, but their planned route to our fallen friends would take them through the location of the secondary IED.

That would be a disaster.

Even Warriors would be susceptible to the molten blade of a shaped charge or copper fist of an EFP. We were sending our own men to their deaths, and in a few minutes we would have completed the enemy's task for them. As we stood in the Ops room three Warriors were charging towards a bomb with no idea of the danger they were in.

'NO! STOP THEM!' I yelled across the Ops room, as confused faces turned toward me. 'They're going right through the secondary! We have no idea what it is and they could be fucked if they go near it.'

I had no authority to stop that patrol – it was Dillon's call. I looked at him.

'Stop them,' he said. 'They will set up a cordon at Red Two near the power station that's about 100 metres away from the secondary. They are to stop any other friendly forces or locals entering the killing area.'

Thank God we had caught them in time. Dillon was decisive

and made things happen quickly. If he had waited another minute we could have lost yet more men; the day was tough enough already.

As the radios burst into life again I imagined the Warrior tracks locking and stopping the 24 tonne monsters instantly, the front dipping and the back rising off the ground with the force of the brakes. In the back, soldiers would slide toward the turret before being thrown back toward the rear door. As they cursed loudly they would have no idea how close they had come to being blown apart themselves.

In their new location at Red Two, commanders dispatched the seven soldiers in the back to search around the vehicles for other IEDs. If the area was clear, troops would then take up defensive positions around the Warrior, some walking around talking to locals in pidgin Arabic while some burrowed into the ground to take up positions as snipers, peering through their telescopic sights at high flats or suspicious men hanging around the contact point, all the time passing information back to their commander.

'Flats, 300 to our north west, movement top left window. Two men observing the ICP.' The sniper spotter relayed the image for his partner whose finger rested on the trigger.

'Roger.– keep a bead on them.' Two clicks left on the sight of their telescopic sight and the window was in perfect focus. They were now the prey as the sniper muttered under his breath.

'Come on, you cunts – just fucking try it.'

We still could not find the REST team. I was getting irate and had only a few minutes before I would leave. I glanced nervously at my watch and, out of earshot of anyone else, cursed them.

I needed to phone John, the SAT in Basra, and tell him exactly what was going on. I might need his advice later if things got tricky. He could hear the terror in my voice as

I repeated everything I knew. It didn't take long: two guys were dead, and I was the only person in Al Amarah who stood between the second device and more death that day. John had served for over twenty years as an ATO and was vastly experienced; he had won my respect with his straight-talking professionalism and would be a great sounding board when things got tough.

It terrified me when he, too, sounded scared.

'Right, Sir.' His soft Northern Irish lilt audibly fought for control. 'You've had a good tour so far, but this is big – this is the one that matters.'

Oh fuck. Even John thought this was a big deal. I went cold. My stomach felt as if someone had tied it in knots. His last words of comfort scared me to the core:

'Don't let your team see any bodies. You're paid enough; you do it.'

He was absolutely right, but I hardly needed reminding that out there somewhere lay two of the Battle Group. As well as defusing the bomb I had a responsibility to my team and their families. If I could protect them from seeing torn flesh, cold eyes or experiencing the smell of death, I would. I was the officer and it was my job.

'Good luck; stay safe.' John always says these words at the end of any email and every phone call. But this time it felt very different.

I had never seen a body, never been to a funeral and had certainly never lost comrades in combat before. Today was going to be quite a day.

Dillon told me I would be escorted out by Sergeant Major Tam Russell and his team from D Company, The Highlanders. This was great news; he was a superb soldier who would move heaven and earth to get us to the scene; exactly the kind of man I wanted on the ground with me. He was equally feared and loved by those in D Company, his effortless natural leadership style bringing absolute loyalty from everyone under his command.

I left the Battle Group Ops room and jogged towards my team, ready by the vehicles parked outside the Ops room. A Warrior screeched through the front gate and slammed to a halt in front of me. I recognized the commander as Corporal Stevie Russell, a young, wiry Highlanders section commander who was one of Tam Russell's men and who had worked with us on many tasks. He had just returned from the scene, his face filthy with a combination of diesel fumes and Iraqi air. And he looked absolutely done in.

Stevie took off his goggles as I clambered up the Warrior bar armour toward the turret, grabbing the smoke discharges as my feet slipped. I needed to know everything I could before leaving camp, but there was only one thing at the front of my mind.

'Who's dead?'

'Dunno.' He shook his head and wiped away the layers of filth from around his mouth. 'But someone on the net said one of them was Captain Holmes.'

I nodded slowly, thanked him and walked to the back of the Warrior before jumping off into the sand below. As Stevie sped away I looked at my team waiting expectantly by the vans and felt almost sick. Rich. I could see him laughing as he left me to defuse the grenades at the police station: 'You're the ATO – good luck!' How could he be dead?

He was supposed to be spending the day hosting the *Panorama* TV crew. He couldn't have been killed. This wasn't a house search, an arrest operation or a deliberate attack on an enemy position – this was hosting some journalists; an easy day. I went numb as I remembered that the *Panorama* crew had replaced my team on the patrol. Were we alive due to a stroke of luck?

I couldn't believe it. Soldiers like Richard Holmes don't die, they can't. No one in their right mind would take them on.

Contact IED.

Rich hadn't been taken on by a soldier; he had been felled by an IED. The coward's sabre.

With heart pounding, mind still spinning I was minutes from leaving on one the most dangerous tasks of my life and my team needed me to lead them into this battle and safely out again. I tried desperately to snap out of my daze.

Jay jumped out of the back of the van, looking furious; he slammed the door shut and stood with his hands on his hips, staring at the vehicle, the road, me and then the road again. Fitzy, Claire and AJ, our driver, looked at me waiting for guidance. This was a crucial time, the time to show them how certain I was that I would get them back to camp safely. I took a deep breath and strode toward them.

Jay joined the group facing me. I contemplated not telling them about Rich, then dismissed it. I'd want to know. Besides, if I didn't tell them, and then they saw his body they might be so shocked that they would freeze and be unable to perform.

As I got closer they looked increasingly concerned. Even before I opened my mouth my eyes welled with tears.

'OK guys.' I waited as Claire received a message on the radio. All eyes were now burning into me. 'Bad news.'

My voice cracked as I spoke.

'It looks like Captain Holmes may be dead and that there is definitely a secondary device out there. But that won't stop us going out there and doing a fucking good job. This is going to be tough, but we'll get through it together.'

The news hit my team like a sledgehammer. Like me, they had worked with Rich, knew him and admired him greatly. To make things worse, someone else had also died, and we would only find out who that was when we got to the scene. One by one, they began to look like I felt and I was overwhelmed with the agony of guilt. I had transmitted my fear to them: they could see it in my face and were now just as scared as I was. A good commander shouldn't show weakness. To this day I still feel guilty for failing that test.

It was now 1055 and we were still waiting for the REST team. There was no sign of them as the Warriors in front revved their engines and commanders conducted last minute checks. I resigned myself to leaving the REST behind and ran to Jay's vehicle. I saw Jay walking towards me and could see how upset he was. Anger had given way to tears which increased as he spoke:

'The Wheelbarrow's fucked. It won't work. The batteries aren't charged, and it won't fucking work.' I couldn't find the words to speak. Jay shook his head. 'I'm so sorry.'

It wasn't his fault: we had reported the problem months ago – to no avail. Our DIY efforts had kept us on the road for weeks but now it had failed. I could see that it had hit him hard. Jay was the Number Two Operator: it was his job to ensure that all the equipment was serviceable and ready to go at a moment's notice. He stumbled as he spoke.

'I . . . I am just so sorry.'

The Wheelbarrow was vital. From this point onwards I knew that if there really was another bomb there, I would have to walk up to it and disable it with my own hands. My life expectancy had just dropped through the floor.

The British Army has spent decades improving the provision of robots to its bomb disposal teams: millions of pounds have been spent developing them to the point where they can climb stairs, view bombs with multiple cameras, cut wires and 'disrupt' or destroy IEDs with highly pressurized water jets. My version of this robot, the Wheelbarrow Mk 8b, was one of the most advanced in the world, and now it was useless.

As I took this information in, I paused and replied with all the courage I could muster at that time. 'Well, we'd better man the fuck up and go and earn our money then, hadn't we.'

I slapped him on the back and watched as he jumped into his seat and gave me a nod followed by a thumbs up. I nodded back and forced a smile. He was the best in the business and now, because we had been given duff equipment, he had the weight of the world on his shoulders. The poor bastard.

We mounted up; Fitzy and I in the lead bomb van were third in the convoy behind two Warriors. They would be our armoured escort into the town and provide protection whilst we were on task. Jay and AJ were just behind us in the second van, while Claire jumped into the back of a Warrior. I flicked the PRR on and brought the mouthpiece to my lips.

'This is it, guys. We've had rockets and bombs galore but this is where we can make a real difference. There are guys out there who are injured, terrified and need our help.' I paused: 'We can fucking do this. Let's get out there, do our job and bring our friends back.'

I wished I believed a word of it.

As we followed the Warriors toward the gate I saw the REST team running around the corner, dragging kit behind them and screaming at each other before jumping into the last Warrior. They had just made it.

7. THE LONG ROAD TO AL AMARAH

28 February 2006

With the REST finally on board, our convoy crawled towards the front gate and quickly ground to a halt. With only a PRR radio I could hear nothing from Battle Group Ops, only the chatter between sentries guarding the camp. We needed to get moving, so I climbed out of the truck and ran towards the front Warrior. There was confusion over what had happened on the ground – no one was sure of the situation and there was disagreement about our route in Ops. This was agony; a huge convoy of armour and bomb disposal assets sitting still, useless, while arguments raged over the safest way for us to get to the scene.

Finally Tam Russell appeared from his turret and gave me the thumbs up, his engines roared and I barely had time to clamber into my own vehicle before the convoy took off at top speed. Warriors crushed small sand dunes and slid over large potholes, while my own vehicle flew off the smallest bump and crashed into dried puddles and damaged tarmac.

Fitzy and I ricocheted around the cab, clinging to whatever we could as we tried to keep pace with the lead Warriors. Behind us, Jay and AJ braced themselves as they saw my own vehicle punished. We drove almost blind. The dry, fine dust thrown up by the Warrior tracks coated our windscreen and caused thick dust storms which we blasted through regardless; nothing would stop us getting to our friends.

After 200 metres of this rollercoaster the dust cleared and the 'Golden Arches' came into view; one sharp left turn later we hit the tarmac of the MSR, Route 6. Behind us, above our route from camp, a thick cloud of dust still suspended in mid air was testament to the speed of our exit from camp. Now on the MSR, I could see the town ahead of us, the edge of which was marked by the imposing prison which stood like a medieval fort guarding the town on the west side of the road.

Immediately behind me in the convoy was the RSM's Warrior. His place could have been in the Ops room, shipping out more ammo or preparing for the return of casualties, but that was not for this RSM. WO1 (RSM) Cammie Gray's men were in trouble: they needed as much help as possible and people with experience like his would be critical on the scene. The thought of staying in camp hadn't even crossed his mind.

A thousand scenarios played out in my mind – had the patrol been hit by a suicide bomber? Was Rich really among the dead? What about the secondary bomb – what would its arming and firing switches be? If it was a command wire I could just cut it with an explosive weapon or even my pliers and get off the ground quickly. If it was victim operated, say a pressure pad or tripwire, I would have no need to walk up to it – I could just shoot at it with my rifle or the Warrior chain gun. I wouldn't risk my life on a manual approach if I already knew what it was and could get rid of it quickly.

My desire to 'see some action' suddenly seemed incredibly naive, draining away in the face of reality. I just wanted to get there, pick up our friends' bodies, make the area safe and get the hell out of there as quickly as possible.

Fitzy glanced across at me every few seconds. He was driving us around the many brick chicanes and deep holes in the road but was most concerned about the welfare of his boss. He understood perfectly the enormity of the situation we were heading into and he needed me to perform. My decisions could determine whether he lived or died, and right now, as he looked at me sitting silently, eyes fixed on the road ahead, he didn't fancy his chances.

A veteran of many IEDD tasks, even Fitzy was scared and anxious, realizing that this task was different. We had lost a friend, there was at least one more bomb at the scene and I was not coping well. The journey to Al Amarah must have felt like a lifetime to him; the combination of death and fear of the secondary device was a potent mix that we felt acutely. I looked back at the road as we began to slow down.

Traffic.

We joined the back of the gridlocked traffic and stopped dead. Locals stood by their cars and peered into the distance to see what the holdup was as their children fidgeted impatiently in the back seats, the intense heat increasing the frustration and anger of everyone in the queue.

I screamed at the front Warrior to get moving. It was not their fault of course, but I wanted them just to bounce all the cars out of the way, even if that was not really an option. I had been on dozens of tasks before this day, in Germany, England, Northern Ireland and Iraq, but none of them had been this important: I had never lost a friend before. There was only one man within hundreds of miles who could defuse the secondary, who could make it safe to recover our friends' bodies and who could work out how to stop this happening again. And that one man was me.

Tam Russell's Warrior grunted as it tried to free itself from its cage of traffic. Shifting back and forth, slowly turning anti-clockwise, creating room for itself, finally roaring as more space became available and it lurched forward at a great rate of knots.

I would only find out later that Tam and Rich were good friends who shared a huge respect for each other. No amount of traffic was going to stop Tam from getting to the scene that day, even if – as on this occasion – it meant balancing his 24-tonne Warrior on the central reservation, standing in his turret and pointing the route ahead like an invading Roman emperor.

If I was in trouble I would want Tam Russell to come and get me. That man would walk through flames and over broken glass and never once think about his own safety. I, like his men, would follow him anywhere and we duly sent the entire convoy up the road, balanced precariously on the central reservation. At the front of the convoy Tam stood proud of his turret, eyes focused on the road junction ahead, which was marked by a huge water tower to its west.

The traffic gave us one advantage; there was less chance of another bomb en route. The insurgency needed the support of local people and would lose it in an instant if they killed Iraqis whilst targeting UK forces. I had never been so pleased to see cars nose to tail in my life.

Our route took us through the centre of Al Amarah, where on other tasks we had been excited to be out doing our job, looking forward to mixing with the locals and enjoying the buzz of being on the streets. All the places we passed were familiar, all the sights and sounds were the same, but the feeling was so different. We were going into combat. We reached the centre of town and turned left, leaving the gridlocked traffic. We had reached the red route, and in the distance, only a few hundred metres away, Red One became visible.

It was carnage.

Even at this distance I could see chaos unfolding before me. Soldiers ran in all directions to find cover and those who could take up protective positions crouched behind armoured vehicles, cars or buildings. Some stood, some lay prone and some kneeled, their fingers clutching the trigger; but all wore the same expression of fear and determination.

Commanders screamed instructions at their men and hundreds of locals stood in groups, some only 10 or 20 metres away from the cordon. Most of the locals were as deeply shocked as we were, but some, a significant minority, were chanting, cheering and shouting: they had killed British soldiers and scored a major victory against their occupiers.

Amidst all the activity, the smoke and the noise I could pick out two sand coloured Snatch Landrovers, one crashed into the side of the other in the middle of the road. I caught sight of a flurry of activity around them before the smoke and dust once again obscured my vision. We screeched to a halt.

We had arrived at the scene of the explosion – the contact point – and all hell was breaking loose.

So often at Sandhurst, during training courses and in my mind I had thought of what it would be like to see such a sight, with fallen soldiers and a baying crowd. I had thought of the thrill of combat, how I would finally get to test my steel and see whether I could really call myself a soldier or not. During my time in Iraq I had occasionally lain awake thinking of the kind of tasks I could be called to and how I would handle them. Would I be able to move forward or would I be paralysed with fear? How would I control my team? Would I survive? I thought of other ATOs who had performed incredible acts and wondered how they had coped, whether they were ever scared? I knew that I was petrified, but also knew that, so far, I had gone forward not back. Fight had beaten flight so far.

It was a massive responsibility, but I drew strength from the combined stares of every soldier on the ground.

I climbed from the cab which up until now had insulated me from the atmosphere of hatred and the sounds of conflict. The crowd cheered, screamed and chanted as bullets flew toward the UK forces. We took cover behind a Warrior and while the sniper reloaded, ran to meet the incident commander, Lieutenant Steven Freer, who was tucked in behind his own Warrior. Petrol bombs landed at our feet, and soldiers rushed around with fire extinguishers and jumped under cover as more rounds rained down. We were being fucked over; this mob was bloodthirsty and wished to see more death. I feared they might get their wish.

Before me, two medics tried to load a bloodied, unconscious casualty into their ambulance whilst ducking away from the intense heat of a petrol bomb that shattered against the side of their vehicle, spitting flames in all directions. A Highlander, fresh to the scene, leapt from the top of his Warrior and sprinted towards the ambulance with his fire extinguisher, but was stopped short by three rounds peppering the road in front of him.

Just a few metres further on, three more men, the walking wounded, were being tended by team medics. Blood streamed from the forehead of the one closest to me, a Jock that had been on the receiving end of a rock launched from the crowd and now drifted in and out of consciousness. The second and third were Paras: huge men with pallid faces, whose voices had been reduced to a whisper.

Half a dozen more fires lit the scene, two or three licking lazily along the tarmac road as others burnt fiercely in the pile of detritus that lined the red route. The gentle roar of flames was interrupted by the high-velocity crack of rifle rounds as long bursts of gunfire stitched the ground around our feet. Worse still, two of our friends lay dead somewhere up ahead and if we ever wanted to see camp again, we were going to have to fight our way through an increasingly angry crowd. We were most definitely in trouble.

As I crouched next to Steve Freer, I realized we had stopped only 60 metres short of the contact point. We were well within the danger area for a secondary device: if one detonated we would be both be killed instantly. But the crowd had already begun to gather behind my trucks and there was no chance of them moving further away. They, too, were in danger.

Looking around Steve's Warrior at the contact point I could see clearly where the explosion had occurred. On the right hand side of the road a crater still smouldered. The ground looked charred; the crater was just less than a metre in diameter and half a metre deep, with the markings of black carbon so common in high explosive around its edge. Fucking hell, I could have stood in it and been at knee height. Earth had been thrown in an arc up to 30 metres away from the crater and covered the width of the road. The surrounding area was a rubbish tip, strewn with sewage, garbage and the detritus of life in Iraq. The perfect camouflage.

I struggled to take it in; only minutes earlier, something else had lain on the very spot from where the last tendril of smoke now drifted towards me. Rich had not seen the object and now he was gone. A hole this big could only be caused by a bomb consisting of at least 15kg of high explosive. Never mind whether this was an EFP, shaped charge or claymore, the blast alone would have been more than enough to tear your arms and legs from their sockets if you were close enough. Just a few hundred grams would bring a plane down, a couple of kilos would decimate a car and 5 or so kilos bring down an entire building.

I shook my head, cleared the soot from my eyes and turned to Steve; he was covered in grime, with dry blood encrusted into his webbing. His eyes were empty and he spoke slowly as he described what had happened.

'We'd travelled down this road towards the PJOC to pick up Rich.' He rubbed his eyes, smudging the black soot around his face, the radio which hung on his webbing chattering non stop.

'We went a long route back, not an obvious route, and they still got us.' His head dropped as he spoke. 'We'd only gone through here about 20 minutes before we were hit.' He clearly couldn't take it in. 'We drove south to meet the Red Route and all of a sudden the road went quiet, cars just fucking disappeared off the side of the road. There was an Iraqi police car following us that stopped and waved a few seconds before the explosion. By the time I realized that they were stopping other cars from following us it was too late – the next thing I remember is the explosion.'

I held his shoulder and nodded slowly. Iraqi police, or people who looked a lot like Iraqi police, had set up a roadblock behind the convoy to stop locals getting hurt in the explosion.

Fuck, had the Iraqi police been in on it, too?

Steve's mind was overwhelmed. He looked in deep shock and he had yet to grasp what had happened. He had coped well so far, but had seen too much. Battle Group HQ were not helping, the constant requests for updates continuing to overload Steve going unanswered.

Nevertheless, his information was extremely valuable. It seemed that the enemy had done everything they could to remain unpredictable.

The puzzle started to come together. This device had been put in place in the 20 minutes of the patrol passing Red One and returning over the same spot with Rich on board. Elaborate devices involving hidden command wires and large main charges take much longer to put in place than that. This was a quick but deadly job.

I had to get to the centre of the action. The Snatch vehicles and crater were not far apart: the clues they would provide could save our lives. The only way we stood any chance of defusing the second bomb was to find out as much as possible about the first. It was quite likely that the insurgents would use two similar devices if they had so little time to prepare.

After taking a deep breath I ran toward the crater and passed Dr Rick who was just about leave. I grabbed him. 'Rick, tell me about the injuries. Are they blast, fragmentation? How did they die?'

I shouted above the roar of the mob as more rioters appeared from behind buildings and out of cars. The situation was getting worse.

If I was lucky, his description of the injuries would give me vital clues to the type of IED. Small metal fragments come from grenades; burns come from incendiary devices, dislocated limbs from blast and more traumatic injuries from EFPs.

Rick spewed forth streams of almost unintelligible medical tech speak – he was clinical, even under pressure. I got the gist: 'So, metal fragments, traumatic injuries to the upper torso. Got it, now get back!'

He disappeared into the back of his ambulance and started treating casualties before I had closed the door. More useful information: the metallic fragments may have come from the bomb itself or be bits of the Snatch that had sheared off during the explosion. Equally, they may have come from an EFP.

Often confused with shaped charges, EFPs were designed to destroy tanks and are made primarily of plastic explosive with a copper liner to provide the lethal blow. However, unlike shaped charges, EFPs cause their damage not by forming a molten jet but by sheer brute force.

After initiation, the detonation wave passes through the explosive and strikes the copper liner. The force of the detonation wave on the curved, dish-like liner causes it to collapse in on itself and within a few milliseconds compresses it into a solid metal slug. This slug is then projected forward at velocities of up to 3,000 metres per second, punching through anything in the way. No special physics, no molten jet, just metal flying at seven times the speed of sound. Improvised EFPs like those seen in Iraq also created lots of additional fragmentation, a huge explosive shotgun that was just as lethal.

The crowds had seen the red crosses marked on Rick's ambulance and let it go. When they turned back to us they grew fiercer, edged even closer and swelled in number.

'Motherfucker!' A rifleman shook his bloodied hand and pointed to a cricket-ball-sized rock on the ground. The soldier cursed again as he replaced his left hand on the stock of his rifle.

'That fucker got me.' He gestured toward a bearded man in a long white robe – the dishdash – who stood at the front of the crowd, his hate for us clear from the deadly look in his eyes and his venomous screams.

'I think the cunt's broken my fucking hand. Just give me a reason, ye fucking prick.' He muttered thick Glaswegian threats that were just as menacing in whatever language you spoke. Dishdash man eyeballed the Jock and smirked. His message was clear – the insurgents had won today.

Rick had left a grim trail of bloodied bandages, abandoned breathing aids and other medical detritus. Spreading over the filthy road was a pool of blood, creating a thick, dark stain that found its way into our boots, vehicles and minds. A few metres away a fire blanket had been blown out of the Snatch and lay spread across the tarmac.

I was still 20 metres away from the scene of the explosion and could now see a section of soldiers in a defensive position all around the Snatch vehicles, looking through their rifle sights and scanning 360 degrees.

I sprinted, half bent over to escape the rounds zipping from the top of the flats that clattered loudly against the road. I dived behind a low sand berm as another volley of shots sprayed the road around me.

'Fuck!' I quickly looked at my legs and wiggled my toes. I had not been hit. Next to me Steve Freer's 2IC, Sergeant Spire, who had been in the ambushed patrol, briefly looked up from his radio handset as he briefed the Battle Group on the situation:

'Thank fuck you are here. What fucking took you so long?'

'Traffic.' For a fraction of a second I think he believed I was joking.

Another round cracked over our heads.

Sergeant Spire spoke of the first Snatch being blown up, of them taking small arms fire and of the damage to the vehicles. He had been in the convoy when the bomb exploded and was clearly in shock, sounding drunk or concussed, his voice shaking as he spoke. He had done an incredible job keeping control at all, but I needed more from him.

'I need to get up there.' I pointed at the Snatch vehicles.

'Aye, I thought you were gonna say that.' Spire snorted a half laugh. He had been through so much and yet he would not give in to his fear. 'Follow me then, ATO, and stay fucking low.'

As we jogged forward I remained focused on the Snatch vehicles ahead and the crowd which had doubled in the time I had been on the ground.

'Don't look down.' He pointed to the fire blanket which I had noticed only minutes before. 'That's Captain Holmes.'

I looked.

Visible at the edge of the blanket were para wings and a square blue badge, the mark of 2 Para. The sheet I had barely noticed was covering the body of my friend Rich Holmes. It was true. He was dead. Any hope I had harboured of a mistake now vanished.

So this was Rich? – energetic, lively, funny and utterly like-able Rich? It was almost impossible to reconcile. His was the first body I had ever seen. And he was my friend.

I was going into shock.

I felt light headed, dizzy and struggled to order my thoughts. I had to snap out of it and get back to work: snipers still peppered the cordon and a live device blocked our only route home. This was crunch time; I could either crumble and break down or find the nerve to carry on soldiering. Fight or flight.

I forced my brain into action. I had to force the image of Rich from my mind for a few minutes, needing to think clearly if any of us were going to survive this day. This act, the most difficult thing I had ever done in my life, took every ounce of courage and energy I had.

Fight.

Looking to my right I could see that Rich had fallen in line with the crater. I was so close now that I decided to go straight there; the vehicles could wait. Rich lay covered in dust, beside his shattered rifle, and with his bullets spread all over the road, as I ran past him to the contact point, to Ground Zero.

This was crazy. Everything I had ever been taught about bomb disposal told me that this was almost suicidal: the contact point is the one place you know the enemy have been, the one place they have had time to plant at least one bomb, maybe many more. Secondary devices were planted to target people just like me; amidst all the rubbish and crap it would be impossible to see a pressure plate or tripwire. You never ever go on to a contact point unless you have cleared every inch of the area around it and are absolutely sure there is nothing to catch you out.

That could take hours – I had seconds.

My friend Captain Pete Norton had been severely injured when he investigated an explosion in Baghdad only months before. A vastly experienced operator, Pete had stood on a pressure pad linked to two artillery shells whilst investigating

Improvised Explosive
Device training –
defusing a suicide bomber
at night

Chemical munitions
disposal training –
making safe a World War
II Livens bomb

Northern Ireland – living my dream as ATO Londonderry with Jay (second from right)

Above Al Khala house search – results of search in children's bedroom

Right The parents' bedroom wardrobe, moments after a grenade was dropped at my feet

Me enjoying the Iraqi weather after surviving my first night of rocket attacks

The biggest kid in the playground, en route to the culvert
to disable two large-shaped charges

The culvert – I've got Warriors, Challenger II tanks, helicopters and fast jets protecting me and the team

Wheelbarrow – workhorse of Northern Ireland that found its limitations in Iraq

Shaped charge from the culvert, capable of destroying the most heavily armoured tank

Above Fitzy and Claire take some time out during one of our demolition days at a disused Iraqi range

Left Jay, my right-hand man, sporting trademark bandido moustache

Below At the PJOC on the milk round picking up rockets, mines and IEDs for later disposal

Fitzy on the streets

We need a bigger bergan – anti-tank mines from the PJOC

Lanes of death – providing counter-IED training to the battle group

Oil-tanker bomb – I was busy defusing mines whilst Rich Holmes hopped around in the smoke

Job done! Two tonnes of anti-tank mines removed from the oil tanker

No Wheelbarrows left – I'm about to be surprised by a secondary device on the rocket firing point

Top Red One – my first view of the carnage

Above Rich's Snatch Landrover (centre) and McNeill's Warrior (left)

Right REME 'Wrecker' taking Snatch vehicle back to camp

Private Lee Ellis PARA

Captain Richard Holmes PARA

Camp Abu Naji
memorial wall

A few days after Red One, deploying again onto Sparrowhawk Airfield with REST. I had run out of courage by this point

Sparrowhawk Airfield – leaving my team again to take the 'Longest Walk' towards yet another bomb

My last task. I never wanted to wear the suit again

The Thinking Bomb

The start of my recovery – receiving the George Medal from the Queen

The George Medal

My beautiful wife and me on our wedding day

another crater. If Pete could be caught out, I knew I could be. (Incredibly, even after losing an arm and a leg in the explosion he managed to maintain control of the scene and coordinated the follow-up actions – bravery for which he was awarded the George Cross.)

This time I had no choice.

I frantically metal-detected a few inches ahead of me as I searched a route over the 2 metres of baked mud that separated the road from the contact point. It was little use; there were shards of metal everywhere. My detector beeped constantly and I was taking too much time. I threw it back into the cleared area behind me; my eyes would have to do.

I thought briefly of all the training I had done, of every rule I had learnt and why I deemed it necessary to throw away all the advice I had been given on this task. But this incident was different; it was like no other that I had trained on. In training the Wheelbarrow rarely fails, time was much less of an issue and every task had a safe solution. I couldn't yet see that this one did.

Every patch of disturbed earth around the crater was a threat, every piece of litter potential IED camouflage. There was nothing between me and the crowd other than distance; they were now only 20–30 metres away.

I had put a gun to my own head by being here at all; by getting rid of my metal detector I had practically pulled the trigger. I needed to find bomb fragments – a command wire or PIR casing to tell me how the bomb was initiated and give me vital clues to disarm the secondary.

I dragged mud away from the depths of the crater by hand, desperate to find any evidence of the bomb, and circled the crater looking for signs of a command wire leading towards the flats less than 100 metres away.

There was nothing. All I had was a charred crater, a whole

lot of debris and pandemonium behind me, as the friction between soldiers and crowd grew hotter and hotter. We were a hair's breadth away from all-out war.

I got on the PRR and told Jay I was heading to the vehicles.

'Roger,' said Jay. The ICP sounded like chaos. 'Keep your head down.' I looked over my shoulder and saw Jay man-oeuvring the EOD vans to form a right angle. This would protect the team against blast and allow shelter from the sniper whilst they worked on preparing my tools for the secondary.

I was not prepared for the sight of Rich's vehicle.

Dozens of holes perforated the right hand side of the vehicle. Most were tiny, and had done only superficial damage, but some were much larger, 5 or 6 inches across, and had torn through both sides of the vehicle. The Snatch 'armour', designed to stop stones in Belfast, now flapped impotently in the wind. Beneath the crumpled right wing, a pool of oil, brake fluid and water slowly congealed with sand around the shredded tyre and now oozed down the slight camber of the road.

The fragmentation had shattered each of the windows, their frost-like opacity masking the interior of the Snatch from the crowd on the north side of the road and allowing some dignity to the injured and dead.

On the other side, the commander's door had been thrown open by the detonation, its hinges deformed by the long heave of the blast wave and the instantaneous punch of fragmentation. Inside, I could see that little more than an empty shell remained; the steering column, gearstick and dashboard had been thrown across the road. Only the driver's and commander's seats remained intact.

They'd never stood a chance.

Looking at the holes on the driver's door I noticed that the metal surrounding each entry point had turned a strange colour. Not the dark yellow of the Snatch paint, or the silver shine of the metallic bodywork underneath. The outside of each was coated in copper.

I inhaled sharply.

Copper was the crucial material used in the manufacture of EFPs; even as they travelled at incredible speeds they left traces of material on every surface they touched. There were dozens of holes in the side of the vehicle ranging from the size of a grain of rice to a dinner plate. Just one EFP could produce two or three large slugs, possibly weighing up to a kilogram each, and many small fragments weighing less than a gram. The smallest fragments may be stopped by the bodywork of the Snatch but the largest would not stop for many hundreds of metres and would barely have noticed the Snatch as they passed through it.

The bonnet was mangled and had been thrown up as the blast wave pounded it. The windscreen and drivers window were shattered and opaque. The glass had protected them from the smaller fragmentation but was no match for the larger lumps of copper.

Standing at the commander's door I could see clearly where the larger lumps of copper had exited the vehicle. Two holes, each the size of a fist, had punched through the driver's door. As I traced the path of each copper slug from driver's side to passenger side my eyes fell upon something else. Something which, amazingly, my mind had not allowed me to see until this moment.

A body.

8. MANNING UP

28 February 2006

Someone was still sitting in the driver's seat, motionless, staring straight ahead. His uniform and physique bore all the characteristics of a paratrooper: knee pad, extra pouches, airborne combat helmet and looking tough as nails.

'Lee Ellis.' Sergeant Spire appeared at my side. 'Fucking great guy. I can't believe it.'

I stood looking at Lee for what felt like an eternity. I had spent the last few minutes examining the vehicle in great detail and had not noticed him. Looking towards his seat I could see first field dressings (used to stop blood) and syrettes of morphine. Rick had tried his best but had been unable to save him. I stood frozen to the spot, only 3 feet away from Lee.

'Sir.' A loud Scottish voice woke me from my trance. Tam Russell was running toward me with someone else in tow.

'This is Highlander McNeil.' To his side was a Highlander. His manner marked him out as being young, a teenager, but today his face was pale, filthy and prematurely aged. His eyes looked haunted and he stuttered as he spoke. He had been on the ground all day and had witnessed the explosion.

I stood with my back to the Snatch passenger door as Tam continued: 'He was the driver of the lead Warrior and ... Oh fuck.' Tam's eyes settled a few feet behind me. For half a second he, too, could barely speak.

'Shit.' Tam muttered under his breath, loud enough for me, but not NcNeil, to hear.

He looked at McNeil, who had yet to see Lee behind me, and moved him to the side of the vehicle where he would not see the body. That would be one less trauma for McNeil to deal with.

'This is ATO. He's gonna sort this out. Now tell him everything you told me.'

He took a breath and began.

'I was driving the lead vehicle. When I heard the first explosion, I knew I was supposed to put my foot down, to get the fuck out of that situation.' He was right; the drills were to drive through an attack or ambush at full pelt, regroup and then decide what to do next.

'I had just put my foot down when I saw something up ahead, it was right in the middle of the road – really fucking weird. I have been up and down this fuckin' road a fucking million times and I ain't never seen it before. I slammed the brakes right on and stopped dead.'

Tam jumped in: 'It's a secondary IED – the guys know what they are talking about, and it's blocking our way out of here.'

McNeil continued: 'It's big, about the size of a couple of ammo boxes. It just looked odd. It's the wrong kind of yellow. Everything in this country is fucking yellow but not that kind of yellow.'

His Warrior had stopped 10 metres closer to the secondary than the Snatch vehicles and was now positioned side on to the bomb, offering some limited protection to the Paras who still refused to leave their comrades' side.

I was stunned by his cool-headedness. He had seen an IED and stopped, when all of his training told him to just get out of the kill zone and, in the confusion of battle, had manoeuvred his Warrior to help his mates.

I hoped he was wrong about the secondary – I hoped it was just another piece of Iraqi street crap – but as I looked at him he seemed very sure.

'Do you wanna take a look?' Shit. He really was certain.

McNeil led Tam and me the short distance to the rear of his Warrior and went down on one knee. He peered between the track and the rear road wheel before turning back to us.

'Aye, that's it, in the central reservation, about 60 metres ahead. It's so fucking weird, ATO. I never noticed it until after I braked, but it's right opposite a fucking huge lamp-post with a red flag at the top. None of the other lamp-posts around here have anything on top except that one.'

I took his place and traced the central reservation away from our position. There, on the right-hand edge of the central reservation, was something that just did not belong. Iraqi towns often had piles of rubbish, bricks or sand at the side of the road but this thing was different. It just wasn't right. It *was* the wrong kind of yellow.

Directly opposite the secondary a red flag flapped in the slight breeze. I looked over my shoulder and looked once again to the front, craning my neck to see into the distance. It *was* the only flag.

The ground around the bomb was baked clay, completely flat, with a dusting of rocks. Between the reservation and the road was a kerbstone around a foot high, made of thick, solid concrete. It was difficult to get to, so was unlikely to be a pressure pad, and I could see no command wire which would probably have been visible on the road. If this was a bomb, it was probably either radio-controlled or, more likely, radio-armed and PIR-initiated.

Maybe, I thought, just like the first bomb.

For the first time I had seen my quarry. It scared the life out of me.

'There's something else you need to know, something really fucked up.'

Tam and I turned to McNeill, who continued.

'After the explosion, when I had seen the secondary and slammed the anchors on, an Iraqi Police car sped up the road behind me, straight past me and drove off the road, round the lamp-post and away from the secondary before getting back on the road 100 metres up the road. It was really fucked up.'

Tam and I exchanged glances once again. The evidence was stacking up; the Iraqi Police either had eyes like hawks or knew that the secondary was there. It wasn't just the insurgents we were fighting.

'Right.' I got on to one knee. Over Tam's shoulder I could see the crowd had grown. 'I'm going to grab the REST team, take a long patrol around the device, and see if there's anything else I can learn. Then I'm going down the road to clear this thing and get us the fuck out of here.'

Tam slapped me on the back. 'Good man.'

I called the REST team to my location. This patrol, called an isolation, would let me look all the way around the device so we could confirm that there were no command wires. This would allow me to get a better feel for the ground, how the bomb was placed there and what it was designed to attack.

My watch beeped 1300hrs.

Shit.

I had already been on the ground half an hour and had not even gone near the bomb. There was so much to do; I raced from the Warrior back to the ICP where I met the REST. They were pulling at the bit and ready to go. They were also absolutely fearless and never blinked at the thought of patrolling right through the middle of the crowd who seemed so intent on killing us.

Our patrol took us from the ICP, through the crowd and

around the device. I had to protect the REST as much as possible and never let them get closer to the bomb than about 50 metres. The crowd could barely believe that nine guys would have the nerve and audacity to walk through them and simply stared in amazement as we patrolled.

Each man had a different role: metal detecting, searching for wires or looking for secondary devices. Moving slowly, deliberately, we walked from the ICP in a counter-clockwise direction around the secondary. We stopped frequently to look at the bomb; I knelt and looked through my binos, desperate to see one detail, one wire, anything that would let me defeat this device. Just one more piece of the puzzle might be enough.

Nothing.

I was just wasting time. Behind me the troops were suffering. Shots rang out from the top of the flats to the north of Red One and I could see soldiers diving behind cover. From the singed uniforms and heavy limps it was obvious that we were taking casualties. We had been lucky with the sniper so far; his rounds had fallen at our feet or slammed into the thick steel hung on the side of the Warriors. Our own anti-sniper teams had managed to keep him off target for this long, but it was surely only a matter of time; men would start to fall before long.

'Right, fuck this!' I screamed at the REST. We were nearing the end of the isolation and I had gained nothing. It was time to make the difference I had wanted to make my whole life. I grabbed the PRR:

'Jay, get the suit ready, I'm going to manual this fucker.' Within seconds the suit was dragged from my van, weapons produced and my kit prepped. Jay and I had done this so often that he needed no instruction. I headed straight back to the ICP.

'Right, let's fucking do it. I gathered the team together and we huddled between our vans, the sides of which drummed constantly with the hail of rocks.

'Fitzy, I reckon this is a Radio Control armed PIR-initiated EFP – I need you to look after me on this one.' He said little but nodded slowly.

'Claire, I need you ready to go with your forensic kit. As soon as this is done we will go to the contact point, get any evidence we can and then fuck off, OK?'

She pointed at the bergan by her side: 'Ready boss. It's all in there.'

I carried on: 'AJ, I need you to provide local protection to this ICP. Don't move more than 10 metres away and keep an eye on Jay and Claire. They are going to be too busy helping me to look after themselves – they are relying on you.'

'No problem, boss.'

'Jay,' I paused, 'this is your ICP now. You run this place until I get back. This is your team.'

We had done this so many times, with so many bombs, but now it felt different. Handing over my team was a formality that I had never really thought about before; I always thought I would be coming back. This time I had every chance of being killed. Jay would lead the rest of the task.

He didn't let me down: 'No problem, Capitano. You just concentrate on that bomb and getting us the fuck out of here.'

I stood still as my team buzzed around strapping me into the EOD suit, lifting my arms, turning me around and slowly building up the layers that, even then, would offer miniscule protection against the size of device that lay in wait.

The suit stank of old sweat and dust, and felt as if it weighed a tonne. The 32kg of Kevlar plates conspired not only to slow an operator down but also to massively restrict his movement. With this suit on I was blinkered due to the helmet, could barely move my arms and had no way of getting quickly out of trouble. For all its weight and thick layers of Kevlar armour it wasn't remotely bulletproof. All in all I was the easiest of targets for the snipers lurking behind the clothes that were hung across many of the open windows in the flats nearby. I knew it wouldn't keep me alive, but it might stop me being blown apart.

I shuffled toward the front of the ICP, the scratched visor on my EOD helmet already dripping with condensation as I leant down to pick up my bergan which was loaded with a further 30kg of tools, weapons and forensic kit. As I heaved it on to my shoulders, the fan on top of the helmet whirred loudly and pathetically and failed to clear the mist from the inside of the visor.

Fitzy grabbed my arm and lifted my visor; he couldn't look me in the eye. I had seen that look once already today. 'I can't provide you cover.'

I went numb.

'My ECM is fucked. It keeps cutting out – one second it's on, the next it just dies.' His look matched Jay's when he told me of the Wheelbarrow. 'I don't know what the fuck has happened. I check it every morning and I checked it before we left camp today and it was working fine. I've had problems with the power supply before and have ordered a replacement power lead.' He paused. 'I've asked again and again but never got one. We're due to get it in a week.'

I was going to die.

We had known for weeks that our ECM was malfunctioning. Fitzy and I had both spent enough time demanding that it be repaired, but it had worked during First Parade this morning and had only just given up the ghost. My ghost.

I hoped I was wrong and had misjudged what lay in wait for us, but if my threat assessment was correct, if all my training and experience had led me to the right conclusion, then I would be dead in only a few minutes. My team would see their boss evaporate before their eyes and Al Amarah would turn into a full-scale riot.

Without a Wheelbarrow or ECM, and with shots still ringing out from the snipers that prowled nearby roofs, I had no chance against this device. How could I defeat the PIR if I had no idea in which direction it was looking? How could I protect myself against the radio-control firing-signal switch if I had no ECM? How could the snipers miss when I was moving at a snail's pace in my EOD suit?

I was playing Russian Roulette with only one chamber empty. The odds against us were immense, insurmountable. It was almost impossible. But there was no choice. We couldn't move our friends' bodies and recover their vehicles until I defused that bomb; it would be too dangerous to attempt that kind of recovery with the secondary so close. Added to that, the device was blocking our way out, and no one wanted to fight through the crowd that had blocked the road behind us.

There was also another reason: if we did somehow get past the bomb and make it home without defusing it, some poor Iraqi would be sent to dispose of it and would have even less of a chance than I did. We were here to help the people of Al Amarah, not sentence them to death, and I could never live with that on my conscience.

This was my bomb, my task and my fate alone.

'Fuck it, we're going. If your ECM is only on for ten seconds during the task, that may be all I need. My only chance is you and your van. Just give me whatever cover you can.'

Fitzy didn't flinch: 'Roger that. I'm ready.'

Jay tossed me the mobile phone that had been ringing non-stop throughout the task. John was desperate to understand what was happening on the ground and had called Jay every ten minutes for updates. This time I called him. I needed his help.

Back in Basra, John had screamed at the EOD Ops room to be quiet as soon as the phone rang. He stood alone in the middle of the room as signallers, drivers and the EOD Ops Officer all looked on. The sounds of the crowd rioting behind me, helicopters passing overhead and stones ricocheting off the van next to me were in stark contrast to the absolute silence in Basra. We were being well and truly fucked and all they could do was listen.

'John, I need your permission to manual this. I have no Wheelbarrow or ECM and our only way out of this place is past the secondary. There are fucking hundreds of Iraqis surrounding us and more arriving every minute. If we try and go backwards we will have to fight through the whole crowd. It would be a bloodbath.'

The weight of responsibility on his shoulders was massive. He knew that I had no option, but also that if it went wrong he would have sent me to my death. The longest twenty seconds of my life was spent hiding behind the thin armour of my EOD vehicle as John went silent.

'Do it.' His voice sounded almost helpless. We had been backed into the same corner and knew that it was the right decision, the only decision we could make. But he also knew that the next phone call he got would probably be from Jay.

John continued: 'But for fuck's sake look after yourself and stay . . .'

A round cracked over my head and ricocheted off the 30mm cannon of the Warrior guarding my ICP.

'Is that you getting shot at?' John sounded incredulous.

'Yeah. They've been shooting since we got here.'

'Well get off the fucking phone and stop talking to me then! And for fuck's sake, stay safe.'

9. THE LONGEST WALK

28 February 2006

There was nothing left to do but walk.

Behind me, every fighting man in the Battle Group who could get to the scene had arrived and swelled our numbers; many had crammed themselves into already over-laden Warriors in order to get to the scene. Some had even driven there in Snatch vehicles, disregarding the threat to their own lives. Anything to help their friends. At Red One they patrolled, faced the crowd and some lay still, the movements of their sniper rifles so slight as to be almost unnoticeable.

Each and every soldier knew what was about to happen: ATO would walk to the bomb, defuse it and we could all get out of there with our fallen friends.

'How are you going to get me the fuck out of here if you can't see?'

Jay had lifted up my visor and was now wiping the inside with a piece of blue tissue. We tried to laugh but it was impossible. He had used the same line so many times and always made me laugh, but now I could not. I had quite enjoyed the anonymity of my misty visor; no one could see that I was almost crying with fear.

I turned away from Jay, away from the crowd and away from the rest of my team, and looked towards the Snatch vehicles. The sight of Rich and the knowledge that Lee was only a few yards further on filled me with an overwhelming sadness. I would have to walk right past them on my way to the target. There was nothing else to do but look straight ahead and place my life in the hands of chance.

From my position at the front of the ICP I could see the place where I was likely to die. If I was lucky, my killer would wait until I was close enough to kill me instantly; if it was not to be my day, I would live long enough to see my limbs torn from my body. The world around me would erupt into noise and action, yet I would hear less and less of it.

Twenty-two British soldiers had been murdered on these streets and lots more blood had been spilt by those lucky enough to survive their injuries. I desperately did not want to become number twenty-three, but the thought of being torn apart by a baying mob terrified me even more. I had seen pictures of the two Royal Signals Corporals butchered in Northern Ireland, US soldiers in Somalia and more recently in Baghdad being dragged through the streets and I felt sick.

If there was the slightest glimmer of hope I had to take it. The bomb could fail, my ECM could kick in at the right moment or I could just be really fucking lucky. My friends needed me.

With only seconds to go before I left the ICP, I grabbed Jay and ushered him to the relative safety offered by the side of the EOD van out of view of the mob, snipers and the troops who needed me to succeed. I had trusted him with my life many times before, but now I needed to trust him with something just as important.

'I'm not going to make it through this one, Jay.' I shook with fear at the thought of what lay ahead. Tears rolled down my cheeks as I continued: 'You have to remember a couple of things for me.'

He looked as terrified as I felt.

'I need you to tell my parents that I love them very much . . . and I need you to get a message to Beth. Tell Beth that I loved her and that I will always love her.'

I knew that I was going to die, but could not die today without letting the people that I loved know that I was thinking of them in my final minutes.

It was my selfishness, my passion for adventure that had brought me here to Red One, and my lust for danger that would wreck their lives. I would have done anything to speak to them, if only for a few seconds.

And I needed Beth to know that in my final moments I was thinking of her. I would never be able to hold her hand again and it hurt. A real, physical pain. Or was that just fear?

'You're gonna be OK,' said Jay. He had to scream it: the noise of the mob was getting louder and louder – they could sense that something was about to happen.

His face betrayed his fear, that particular look that occurs only when people are absolutely terrified. Looking into Jay's eyes was like looking into a mirror.

'Just remember my messages.' I looked him in the eye one last time and turned away, towards the bomb.

'Kev.' Jay never called me Kev, always Sir, Boss or el Capitano if he was feeling cheeky. I couldn't move my head inside the suit so turned my whole body to face him.

'You can tell them yourself. You know what to do. You're gonna be OK.'

I half smiled and faced the bomb once again.

Fitzy revved his engine and once again gave me the thumbs up: he was ready to go. I readjusted the heavy bergan on my shoulders and stepped out of the ICP. I had made the hardest step – the first – and was now on my own, only minutes away from certain death.

Then my bergan strap broke.

Scattered across the road were some of the explosive weapons and tools that had been stowed in my rucksack. I looked at the main strap and saw a frayed end hanging freely. This really was a bad day.

A minute later I was repacked and was ready to leave the ICP once more. As I walked past the driver's door of Fitzy's van and directly in front of him, I turned to see him. One nod from Fitzy was the acknowledgement that he was ready. IEDD Operators should always walk behind the van, shielded from blast and fragmentation if the bomb explodes early.

Today was different; I would not ask Fitzy to go closer to the bomb than me. I walked in front of the van. I and my EOD suit would offer little protection to him from the bomb, but it would show him that I was prepared to take the greater risk. Fitzy was my mate. It was the least I could do.

I walked forward alone; on my way to the bomb that I was certain would end my life.

Walking like this is not a subconscious action; every step requires thought, every single movement is controlled.

Step left, step right, kneel. Stop, lift visor, scan. Visor down, stand, step left, step right.

My senses were on fire as I made agonizingly slow progress. My eyes strained to make sense of the fishbowl image presented by the curved visor and re-focused to see past the condensation that the fan failed to prevent. My ears were swamped with engine noise from Fitzy's van behind me and the fan that purred ineffectually on top of my EOD helmet. I struggled to pick out anything but the sharpest sounds as rounds zipped overhead.

The combination of sweat, the horrendous smell of the EOD suit and the more familiar smells of rubbish and burning clay that hung over the city made me want to retch.

My eyes darted on to every object and instantly locked on to any movement from the crowd but most of the time I was looking to my half right. The arc of debris thrown out by the first explosion was a graphic reminder of how my friends died and the explosive power of what lay ahead. There was little dignity for anyone today, but Rich's team had done what they could to look after him. His shattered body lay still. I could look at nothing else as each step brought me closer to him and further away from my team. As I approached him, tears began to stream down my face; soon I was within a metre of him and was crying aloud. Now at his side, I paused for the briefest of moments and looked at my friend.

There was no fucking way I was going to let him down today, no fucking way. I could get turned into red mist, blown apart or thrown across the road by the blast but I would not stop going forward. It would only get tougher and more terrifying as I got nearer the bomb but from now on there would be no question of whether to carry on.

I would fight, every single time.

I pushed away thoughts of Rich and suppressed the crippling fear that sought to strangle my body as tears streamed down my face. For a second the fatigue and horror of the scene disappeared as I thought of Rich's smile, a huge grin that had won him so many friends and was so frequently seen as he donned his body armour and went to work with his beloved Paras.

I saw Lee again just a minute later. I had never met him, but knew he had chosen to join the Army and was considered tough enough to be a Para. And that he would have had friends and family who loved him. I briefly hesitated as I thought of Lee, but could not stop because I knew that if I did I might never move forward again.

The fear I had tried hard to suppress flooded back with a vengeance. There was now nothing between me and the bomb, no protection from the blast or sight of what lay ahead. I thought of my parents briefly, but then had to force even them from my mind. If I could keep going forward and go against every instinct in my body, there might be a tiny chance that this could work, that we could all get back to camp, regroup and come back to kill the people who had done this to two of our own.

It has often been said that bravery is not the absence of fear, but the ability to overcome it. It is not for a man to judge how brave he is, but I know that at this point I was terrified. Nevertheless, something made me move forward. It wasn't bravery; I just couldn't let my friends down. My friend lying in the Iraqi dust, poor Lee in his seat, and all of my fellow soldiers who relied on me to clear the route to camp. The day had gone on long enough.

There are only a few moments in my life when I have been completely focused, so engrossed in the moment that everything but my own feelings, intellect and emotion was non-existent. The last time had been during the terminal screech of a 107mm rocket.

As I walked toward my death, the raging mob disappeared and the brave men guarding me were forgotten. For those few minutes, I was completely alone, the only person on the planet, and about to do something that every part of me knew was suicide. Every instinct screamed at me to turn back – fight tomorrow not today. But this was the right thing and I couldn't let Rich and Lee down.

Fitzy had come far enough. I pointed to the ground and mouthed, 'Here.' In a well-rehearsed routine he jumped out of the cab, ran to the back door, climbed inside and slammed it shut behind him. Inside he would be met with walls covered in lights, rows of extra ECM equipment blinking in the half light.

Left step, right step, stop. I placed the bergan down, knelt and pulled out my binoculars. Visor up, I examined every inch of ground between me and the bomb, and then the bomb itself.

I had yet to catch my breath and the view in my binos jogged in time with my chest rising and falling.

The wind picked up as I looked ahead, and tiny dirt devils swept around me. Through the binos I could see that the bomb was covered in some kind of material which now flapped in the wind. Even this presented a threat to me. If I got close and this material covered the PIR, it would detonate without me having put a foot wrong. The presence of this loose fabric was also a surprise; most bombs in Iraq were covered with the expanding foam used in building insulation. After the foam set the whole device would be rolled in damp dirt and left to dry. The result would be IEDs that looked just like rocks – the perfect camouflage.

The insurgents had slipped up here. With so little time they had not matched the camouflage of this bomb to the surrounding area and McNeil had seen it just in time.

With a twist of the binocular lens I zoomed in and could now see every detail on this side of the bomb. Again I searched for a wire, a battery, a weak point, a link in the circuit that I could break.

Juicy targets like that were not uncommon in Iraq. The insurgents had to arm them somehow and often left two loose wires at the back which would be twisted together to complete the electrical circuit. They would then retire to a safe distance and arm the device using a mobile phone, car-key fob or whatever other piece of radio equipment they could afford.

If I saw a wire I could cut it from 10 or 20 metres away with my stand-off disruptor. Just load the weapon with my 'Dagger', a super-sharp scalpel, point the laser at the wire, stand back and hey presto. We could all go home.

There was no wire.

10. THE BOMB

Somewhere on that bomb sat the PIR. I had no idea where it was or in which direction it was pointed; only that it sat there, never tiring, just looking, waiting for a target. Glued to the front of the Fresnel lens would be a small black rubber disc with a 10mm hole cut through the centre of it. This small hole allowed only the narrowest field of view for the PIR and ensured when it did detect a person or vehicle there was no way it could miss.

I assumed that the bomber planted this device in the hope of hitting another vehicle. They had seen our drills often enough to know that we accelerated away from contacts and they now planned ruthlessly to exploit our pattern. If this was the case, the PIR was most likely to be looking north, straight across the road.

If McNeil had not reacted so quickly his vehicle would have been first into the firing line, the blast initiating at the front left of the vehicle, right next to the driver's seat. McNeil would have taken the brunt of the detonation, his exposed head only a metre away from the bomb. The Warrior commander would also have been sprayed with supersonic fragmentation and would have been very lucky to survive. As for the gunner and seven troops in the back, only the Warrior armour stood between them and death. Thank God we trained our soldiers so well. McNeil had saved his and others' lives with one quick decision.

My route straight along the central reservation seemed to be the least likely place the terrorists would target. They expected the target vehicles to drive on the road, not the reservation. My shoulders sank. I was walking toward one of the most sophisticated bombs in the world and I was relying on an educated guess for survival.

I moved slowly and I moved predictably, the perfect target for a sniper. The same man who had been seen firing at us from a rooftop earlier was still alive, and would love to take a bomb disposal man. We were high value targets which would mean a big pay day if he could kill me. I had left behind the security of my ICP and the reassuring mass of Warrior and was now completely exposed. If he wanted to, the sniper could take my head off with a single round. Maybe he was playing games or had taken pity on me, but I had made it to within 30 metres of the bomb and had so far got away with a few near misses.

I had now entered the IED's killing zone; at this range I did not even want to see the PIR. If I saw it, it would see me and it would react a lot more quickly than I could. I was also close enough to be killed should the terrorist detonate the device remotely, or if a stray round from those shooting at me struck the device. Shit, I would be killed even if one of the stray dogs that prowled these streets decided to have a piss near the bomb.

Thinking back to the wise words given to us on the first day of my IEDD course I almost laughed aloud. I had found it. This was the 1 per cent terror.

I wished I had listened more intently at the Felix Centre, where I was always criticized for carrying too much kit to the target. The exertion of carrying my own bodyweight in EOD suit, tools and ECM kit had already brought me to the brink of exhaustion and I still had the really difficult bit left.

Now only 20 metres out, I looked through my binos again. There must be something there, something I could attack. Without seeing a weak point I had few options; if I fired blindly I would just do the terrorist's job for him and initiate the device; and there were Iraqis close by who might be killed by it. I would never take that risk: not only would it be a tragic waste of life, but more blood would be spilt in the minutes, days and weeks that followed.

Somewhere in the crowd I imagined a man waiting. He stood towards the back of the crowd, out of sight of the Battle Group but with a good view of the road. He caused no trouble, threw no stones and had no other weaponry nearby. With both hands thrust into the pockets of his thin jacket, his right hand would be wrapped around a small plastic container the size of a cigarette box. As his thumb ran over the surface of this object it would reach a row of three buttons. Each had a tiny plastic sticker underneath, with simple instructions written in clear English:

Arm
Disarm
Fire

It was the third button that he had yet to press. This was the culmination of a long day and in a few minutes it would be over. I imagined him waiting, his hand on the electronic trigger, begging, urging me to get just that bit closer. And as soon as I did – he would kill me.

In the darkness of his van, Fitzy would be desperately trying to jam the firing signal. He was good, very good, but his chances of success were pitiful as the power light of the ECM flashed intermittently on and off. My life hung by the thinnest of threads, all for want of a £10 power cable.

Poor Fitzy. Although he was halfway between me and the ICP he was still right in the firing line. This wasn't just about protecting him; he had a gorgeous wife, Danielle, two wonderful kids and was a great husband and father. I didn't want to let them down either.

My final steps toward the device grew even more surreal. I was *there*. How could I get this close? The object before me had been created with one purpose, to kill British soldiers; and now one was edging closer and closer.

My first bomb disposal task had brought a similar state of surrealism. A man had dug up a grenade, placed it in a bucket, walked into a nearby police station and promptly put it on the desk. Nearby houses were evacuated and the bucket moved to a school field where a secure cordon could be put in place. After driving at full pelt to get there, sirens blaring, I walked up to the bucket to see exactly what was waiting for me and felt the same kind of dreamlike haze as I realized that it was indeed a real grenade and potentially lethal.

That was a long time ago. Everything seemed a long time ago as the red flag fluttered mockingly to my right.

The pungent smell of burning rubbish quickly brought me back to Al Amarah. My mind was in overdrive, lost in a thousand different thoughts. Where was my team? How close were the mob? How could I defuse the bomb? Where was my shadow? Was it near the PIR sensor?

Left step, right step, watch the shadow, left step, right step, stop. Close now, get on to your front and crawl. Only 50 centimetres to go. Crawl more slowly.

I was right next to it. I had beaten the PIR. How was I still alive? Why hadn't they just pressed the button and claimed more British blood? Why had the sniper spared me?

The bomb, my nemesis, lay just a few inches from my face, the size of two ammo boxes, the wrong kind of yellow and covered in hessian. As the fabric flicked in the breeze I caught glimpses of the yellow expanding foam underneath, which was the right kind of yellow. Inside lay one, maybe two steel cylinders, only a few inches across but packed with enough C4 to kill most armoured vehicles. A small electronics pack would be hidden somewhere, maybe towards the rear of the device, from which electric cables would lead towards a shiny detonator, one inserted into the back of each EFP.

I knew intimately how these devices worked; I could attack any part of the system with a simple pair of pliers, pull the detonators from the back of the EFPs, untwist the arming wires or even target the electronics pack itself. I had spent so long studying IED electronics that I knew the function of every resistor, capacitor and programmable chip off to a tee.

If I could get to them.

The insulated foam coated every surface of the bomb and although it had been sprayed from an aerosol can, it quickly hardened into a tough plastic. I could cut through, but it would take too long and the risk of jolting the device would be too high. I had come too far to take stupid risks now.

I wouldn't just blow it apart: there was too much to be learned from gathering all the components together for that. If we were to stop more British deaths in this town I would need to understand exactly how the first bomb functioned, and those answers lay within the object in front of me.

After all my theoretical training, all my experience, all the advice I had taken from other EOD operators, it had come down to this. The next minute would define my character, my skill, my luck and the rest of my professional life. If I succeeded, I would have been able to help my friends, my fellow soldiers and would have done my bit. If I failed, my parents would never see me again: they don't let relatives see bodies if they are completely disfigured. I was too close to this device to get away with any mistake.

I had already spent too long next to the bomb; Fitzy in his ECM van would be desperately trying to guard me against all of the incoming signals aiming to detonate the device. Back in the ICP, Jay would be keeping one eye on me and also trying to organize my team, keep control of all the EOD weapons and look after himself, the poor bastard.

The choice of weapon was critical. Too much power and the device would evaporate, along with all the forensic evidence that clung to sticky tape, on plastic surfaces and even in the explosive itself. If only I could bring the bomb back intact, teams of ATOs and scientists could pore over its every detail and extract every nugget of information about its capabilities and the bomb-maker. If we could do that we might catch the killers and the risks would have been worth it.

If the weapon was not powerful enough, the bomb would just get angrier, even less predictable and I would have to walk up to it all over again.

One weapon, Sliver, would separate the components without detonating the explosive, rendering it safe but not destroying it. Sliver was a great piece of kit but had to be positioned within a few millimetres of the bomb to function correctly. I would have to slide a couple of inches further forward than I was already in order to finish the job.

The thick EOD suit crippled me as I fought to manoeuvre my arms to position the weapon. I lay on the thick armour plate which formed the front of the suit and my visor scraped along the hard ground as I inched Sliver across the ground, 3 or 4 millimetres at a time, constantly checking its proximity to the device and the fall of its shadow, and urging myself to get it just that bit closer. After coming all this way, the very last thing I needed was to nudge the bomb now.

Somehow my educated guess on which direction it was looking had paid off and allowed me closer than I had thought possible.

Just a few more millimetres. A small stone skipped forward from the bottom of the weapon and struck the hessian. I froze.

Just a few more millimetres.

I glanced at the crowd to my right: any one of them could now be reaching into their pocket and wrapping their fingers around the radio-control transmitter. My killer could be a man, a woman, young or old, and was probably looking at me right now. Whoever it was had probably been watching Rich's convoy as it approached the contact point, had seen my manual approach and any second now would press the plastic button that would end my life. I would be the only person in Red One who wouldn't hear the explosion.

My heart raced as I slowly removed my hands from the edges of Sliver, now in the perfect position to be unleashed against the bomb. My finger moved back slowly, careful to avoid nudging the weapon, tracing the wire connecting Sliver to the firing pack back in the ICP. I had seen dozens of operators get caught in these wires and unwittingly walk back to the ICP dragging weapons and Bergans in their wake. Sweat fell from my chin as I slowly stood up, checked the weapon one last time, backed away a few steps and turned.

It was set: I had done everything I could to protect my friends, my colleagues and even the mob who wanted us all dead. It was time to return to Jay and get this threat off the streets.

Maybe I should have run away from the device, used every last scrap of energy to leave its kill zone, but I did not. I walked deliberately, carefully, along the same path that I had used to approach the device, watching my feet and ensuring that the firing cables stayed well away from me. The first 10 metres were agony as I continued to wait for the intense heat and light of the bomb finally detonating, but it never came. As it became more distant I felt elated, the highest of highs finding more reserves of energy to propel me away from danger.

Taking in the scene ahead of me, I was struck by the rest of the Battle Group. I had barely thought of them during my manual approach, but while I was trapped in my own world of fear they had seen rounds skipping off the road beside them, flames erupting on the side of their vehicles and the crowd close in even more. Still they maintained security, looked after their friends and kept the mob at bay.

My feeling of isolation disappeared as the familiar faces of the team poked out from around the back of the van. Being so focused on the task had completely distorted my perception of time. I thought I had been out only a few minutes, but the 20–30 minutes I had actually spent walking up to the bomb must have felt like hours as they waited for the inevitable loud report of the EFP functioning. As I got within 20 metres of the ICP I found no energy to be elated or scared. As the feeling of terror ebbed away, exhaustion began to fill the vacuum.

I had only walked a few hundred metres, but so much adrenalin had been used that I now had almost no energy left at all. I could feel every gram of the suit's armour and was a physical wreck when I reached my team. They tore the suit off me and I felt as if I was floating, such was the relief at losing the burden. My combats had turned dark with sweat and clung to my body.

There was no time to relax; now in the ICP I began to command again, to ensure that everybody was safe for the imminent explosion. As well as all of the soldiers, I had to ensure that no Iraqis were close to the device or in direct line of sight of it.

Timing was critical: I had to be certain that no one would

be injured if the bomb did detonate, that the sky was clear of aircraft that may inadvertently get shot down by my explosion and that all the Brits got behind armour. Just as importantly, we had to make sure that all of the Iraqis were well away from the kill zone. If I hurt someone in the crowd, we would never leave the battlefield that day.

Men huddled behind armour, vehicles closed their hatches and anyone who could do so found the nearest wall or ditch to shield themselves from the blast.

I was happy, and told Jay to get on with it.

He attached the Shrike firing device to the cables that led to the weapon and looked around one last time to check that everyone was out of the way. Grasping the Shrike with both hands he pressed the large rubber button, charging the firing capacitor. When he pressed the red 'fire' button, the capacitor would dump its current down the firing cable to the Sliver detonator and then ... well, then we could all go home.

The firing sequence was simple, it mattered not whether we were blowing up a hand grenade or the most sophisticated device Al Qaeda had to offer, always 'Standby ... Firing!'

Jay was ready, everyone knew what was about to happen.

'Standby ... F– STOP STOP STOP!' he screamed. 'There's a fucking helicopter!'

I looked up. In the glare of the sun I could see that one of our own helicopters had moved overhead. If the device had detonated, we could have brought the heli down and killed our own people.

Tam screamed into his radio, the heli banked sharply and flew over the stadium to the south where it hovered as it waited to land and pick up Rich and Lee.

'Standby ... Firing!'

The loud BOOM echoed off the flimsy walls of the flats nearby and a tall tower of black smoke appeared from where

I had left Sliver. For a few seconds the crowd remained absolutely silent. So did I, as I listened for sounds of screaming, reports of casualties or any indication whatsoever that I had fucked up and hurt someone. Most bomb disposal men can face the possibility of death, but the thought of hurting anyone else was not something we could contemplate.

As the echoes subsided and the smoke drifting away over the flats gradually dispersed, the crowd began to shout, scream and cheer. More excited than angry, they had seen an explosion, were all safe and knew that we would be leaving as soon as we could.

My job was far from done. Although the explosion was loud and the smoke a good indication of success, I could not be sure that the area was safe until I had seen it myself, not least because we needed to drive through it to get back to camp.

I had taken the suit off and had no plans to don it again for this approach. Consumed by fatigue, I was too hot, too tired and could not afford the time to put it back on or wait the mandatory length of time before walking again. This delay is supposed to act as a defence against any electric detonators that had yet to function but had to be balanced against the risk of the still-present sniper.

Jay was furious.

'If you aren't going to wait then you must wear the suit.' He had just seen his boss escape on one approach and was not about to let him go without trying to protect him.

I was too fucked, too exhausted from the last manual approach, and told him so.

This time I took a paratrooper halfway to act as my personal protection. I may not have been wearing my suit any more but felt just as secure having one of these guys look after me. He followed 10 metres behind me, a belt of 5.56mm ammunition swinging from his machine gun, and glared at the crowd.

I doubted very much that anyone would even look at me, let alone try to attack with this kind of support.

As I approached to within 20 metres I could see that the bomb had been disabled, that the components were separated and that the device was no longer a threat. Hessian sacking flapped in the breeze as golfball-sized lumps of insulation rolled down the road toward me. Lumps of C4 explosive covered the immediate area, not a pristine white anymore but dark yellow due to the sand covering every surface. The electronics pack lay just a foot or so further on from the device's original location, slightly charred but largely intact.

Only a foot away from the second crater I saw a small round black object. It looked out of place amongst the other debris and had not been there when I had spent so much time looking around the bomb on my first manual approach. I knelt down, picked up the small rubber object with my hand and immediately recognized it.

The PIR cover. I was right.

This was an incredible find – not only did it confirm my initial assessment but it was within a metre of the device itself. It had probably been blown tens of metres into the air by the force of the Sliver and had landed close enough to allow me to find it. My eyes welled with tears once more as I took on the significance of this small disc. As I peered through the small hole in the centre I wondered whether the PIR had ever seen me, and if so, how the fuck was I still alive?

I threw the disc into a forensic bag. I had beaten the bomb.

In the centre of the reservation were two craters, the smallest of which was closest to me and had been caused by Sliver. Next to it, only 6 or 7 centrimetres further on was a much deeper hole, burned into the ground with a thin black carbon coating. This ground was much harder than the original contact point and I felt sure that the even though this crater was smaller the devices would have been of similar size, about 15kg of C4 explosive.

Job done. We could start to plan getting off the ground. I jogged back to the ICP. Free of the suit, my toolbag and fear, I was elated as I arrived back – I couldn't wait to tell my team that it was over, that they had done well and that we would be back in camp before long. We had only to collect the forensic evidence from the scene and could then get out of there, guarded by the rest of the Battle Group for the drive back to camp. We were nearly there.

My PRR buzzed into life.

'ATO, our call sign to the west has identified a third device, say again a third device.'

I sank on to one knee. Any trace of the elation I had felt after defeating the bomb had vanished in an instant. Now I stared at the dusty road that lay between me and yet another bomb.

I had put myself through mental torture to defeat the secondary device and barely had the energy to stand, let alone go through it all again. I could not believe what I had just heard and simply did not know whether I had the reserves of courage to go back out there once more.

Around me, my team and the cordon troops had also heard news of the third device over the radio and now looked on expectantly. ATO would save the day – he had done it once, surely he could do it again?

But I had nothing left, no energy, no courage, no nerve. I just didn't have it in me to go back out there. The terrorists had robbed me of any courage I had left.

I was moments away from letting down hundreds of people who needed me. The look of disappointment on their faces would destroy me. How could I ever live with the knowledge that, when it really mattered, I had failed?

'FUCK!' To my right a Highlander had managed to jump

out of the path of a Molotov cocktail which now sizzled at the side of the road.

Filthy, hopeless eyes fell upon me as troops searched for a solution, any way they could get back to camp. The enemy snipers had yet to claim a life, but there had been enough ricochets and fragments zipping around to take their toll. The tertiary device was reported to be blocking our way back to camp and, above me, the heli had still not managed to land and take Rich and Lee back to Basra.

We had achieved nothing. And I was finished.

'ATO, confirm my last over.' Shit, they want an answer.

I grabbed the PRR, brought the mouthpiece to my lips and closed my eyes. My life, my view of who I was, would never be the same. I had spent years searching for this moment. I was so fucking naive.

'ATO, confirm my last over.' I found the pressel with my thumb and prepared to break the news.

I looked up, to Jay, who stood at the back of the EOD van awaiting my instruction, and to Fitzy who was ready to climb back into the cab of his ECM van. Then I looked straight ahead, towards Rich and Lee and thought of their families, who were probably not even aware yet that they were dead.

If I did not defuse this device we might never recover their bodies. There could be no funeral, no grieving, no goodbye.

Fuck that. No fucking way.

From nowhere adrenalin once again coursed through my body, my exhaustion disappeared and my mind snapped back into focus. Only the fear remained. I took a deep breath, closed my eyes for one second, jerked upright and heard the familiar white noise as I found the green pressel switch.

'This is ATO confirm location of third device over.' I could do this. I had already cheated death once today and would just have to do the same again.

All around me troops darted to their defensive positions and my team once again flew around the ICP in a blur of focused activity. I gestured to Jay. We needed another Sliver. I had no idea what would be out there and wanted to be prepared. Within a minute I was ready to go. Jay mopped away the condensation from my visor and Fitzy revved his engine, gave me the thumbs up and mouthed 'Let's fucking do it' through the armoured glass and wire mesh of his window. I nodded back and smiled and mouthed back to him: 'Time to man the fuck up.'

He laughed, revved loudly and released the handbrake. It was time to leave again.

The net fell silent for a few seconds – never a good sign. This was going to get worse.

'Sorry, ATO – our mistake – the guys got jumpy and saw some of your equipment in the road, cancel third device over.'

Overwhelming euphoria washed over me as I took in the news.

'ATO, Roger out.' I flicked up my visor and saw Fitzy slump forward in the cab of his van, his head resting firmly in his hands.

It really was done. I *had* beaten the bomb.

11. IMMEDIATE AFTERMATH

28 February 2006

With the device disabled I could now afford to try and take in the battlefield before me. I had seen situations like this dozens of times before at Sandhurst and the Felix Centre, but now found myself overpowered by an onslaught of conflicting emotions: relief at having survived so far, and fury at those who had committed this act.

But above all I felt an overwhelmingly deep sadness – a new sadness, such as I had never experienced before.

Although we were physically exhausted and mentally drained, the day was far from over. Unless I gathered every scrap of evidence, the terrorists who did this would never see justice, either in the courts or at the dangerous end of an SA80 on full auto. I looked at Rich's body, still cloaked by the fire blanket, and still could not take it in. Was that really him? I just couldn't link the man I had known with the body that I had been working around since I arrived on the scene.

At that moment I preferred justice by SA80.

Even worse than that, until I worked out how to stop this kind of IED, the entire Battle Group was at risk.

'Right, listen in.' I shouted above the roar of the Warrior engines as I delivered quick battle orders to the RSM, REST, Tam Russell, WO1 Joe Lloyd (the REME Artificer Sergeant-Major) and my own team, all of whom were crouched around the side of the Warrior, for a minute shielded from the crowd.

'This is fucking critical; if we fuck this up we will never know what happened here today, how to stop it happening again or who did it.'

I paused and looked each person in the eye. It wasn't just me who was fighting to control his own emotions today; every single person looked as if they had been to hell and back.

'Worst of all, we will have let our mates down. So let's do it and get the fuck out of here'

The unflappable RSM grabbed the nearest signaller and was now giving instructions to cordon troops and updating Battle Group Ops. His voice was calm and measured, his orders precise and clear, as if he was on exercise in Sennybridge.

The ASM had already devised a plan to get the damaged vehicles back to camp and was just waiting for Fitzy, who had clambered in the back of Rich's vehicle to check the ECM, to finish, before he could shackle the vehicle to the huge green 'Wrecker' truck. This giant green beast of a machine, manned by the oldest and boldest that the REME could provide, would drag both vehicles back to camp.

I had held Claire back.

I took a breath: 'Claire, I need you to take photos of the scene and everything that gets picked up by REST. But don't go near the front vehicles. Lee Ellis' body is still in the driver's seat and I don't want you to see it. I'll take those photos.'

There was no need to expose anyone else to images that might haunt them. She said nothing.

'Is that alright?' I looked at Claire.

'Fuck off, sir. It's my job and you have a million other things to do.' Never underestimate the professionalism of the British soldier, I thought, as she removed the lens cap, turned on her heel and walked directly to the Snatch vehicle without batting an eyelid.

Tam Russell had waited behind after the O Group and observed my conversation with a wry smile.

'She's harder than a section o' fucking SA fucking S.' Together we watched the fearless Corporal Vogel painstakingly recording every single detail of the scene. Anyone who said that women couldn't hack it on the front line had not met my WIS corporal.

'There is one other task to do, one you didna mention.' Tam looked away briefly before looking right into my eyes. In his late thirties, he had spent a lifetime in war zones and today looked more like 50, the lines around his eyes made even starker by the soot that coated his face. I nodded, slowly.

'Yep. Rich and Lee. What do you think?' I needed advice from someone who had been there and done it too many times.

'I'll do it. I'll secure the HLS and take the bodies to the helicopter. I've known Rich Holmes for fucking years and I want to make sure he gets there OK. He would do the same.'

A few seconds passed as he slowly wiped away the soot from around his eyes; he looked tired and as emotionally exhausted as I felt. His face lacked some of the energy that I had always seen before. Tam often spoke of his hunger for soldiering; I wondered whether there was slightly less hunger in those eyes every time he lost a friend.

Piece by piece the road was cleared of anything that might help the forensic teams in Baghdad and the UK. Jay stood behind the line of searchers as they moved forward through the scene, slowly filling the clear plastic bags with copper fragments, the front fascia of a mobile phone and lumps of C4 explosive.

'You'll need this.' Jay squinted into the sunlight as I held up the small object in my hand. He looked closer, took the black disc into his own hand and rubbed his thumb over its shiny surface.

'Fuckers. You were right.' Jay looked as surprised as I had felt when I first saw the disc.

'Yep, the secondary was a PIR; I'll bet the first device was, too. It was too accurate a hit to be a command wire. They knew they would have no chance against a Warrior and took on the first Snatch in the patrol.'

The heli passed over our heads towards the north-west corner of the Olympic stadium, drowning us out. The telltale pop of a smoke grenade initiating echoed from the monolithic concrete structure moments before the first wisps of smoke spat out.

'It was fucking clinical.' I paused. 'I think we have just found a new bomb team in town.'

Unless we stopped these guys we could expect more of the same.

Jay and I watched in silence as the Merlin helicopter swooped down towards the tall stack of orange smoke that climbed lazily from the grenade towards the heavens, silhouetting the four stretcher-bearers who had arrived only minutes earlier. They crouched as the Merlin descended, the crushing downdraft buffeting them and the smoke, which was thrown back towards the earth, tumbling away from the landing site in all directions. A fifth man stood upright, alone, a few metres closer to the landing site, refusing to buckle against the relentless pummelling of the heli.

Within a minute the Merlin's engines had roared as she lifted and turned south towards Basra, carrying our friends away.

The spent grenade coughed a light trail of smoke at the party of five men who remained at the HLS for a few seconds after take-off. Tam removed his combat helmet and stood watching the heli as it disappeared out of sight over the stadium.

As the thump of the heli receded he crouched down, picked up his rifle and slowly replaced his helmet. As his team headed north towards the ICP he once again glanced south towards

Basra, but the heli was long gone. Grieving would have to wait; there was no respite. It was time to soldier again, to get back to commanding men.

The final preparations were made and our convoy began to move back to camp. The mangled carcasses of the Snatch vehicles hung limply from the huge Wrecker arm as Warriors positioned themselves along the road to cover our departure.

The same men sat in the same positions in the same armoured vehicles but that was all that was unchanged. They had each explored extremes of horror and fear and returned to camp as different men.

There was only one possible route home: straight along the Red Route, on a grim battlefield tour. Within seconds of the convoy snaking away, we were passing the first crater, which had already gained a yellow tinge as small gusts of wind dragged sand on to the blackened earth, grain by grain erasing evidence of the atrocity that had occurred hours before. The arc of earth which had been thrown out by the explosion was now marked with dozens of pairs of footprints and a lone reminder of my friend Rich, the fire blanket lying, discarded, where he had fallen.

The secondary device, my device, came into view only moments later. I thought of how close I had come to death and experienced yet another trough of desperation. Throughout the task my emotions had risen and fallen dozens of times, but I now reached a new low. I took comfort only from the knowledge that neither Rich nor Lee would have known anything about what happened to them – no flash, no bang, no pain, nothing. It would all have been too quick.

One hundred metres west of the secondary was the checkpoint where the QRF had stopped and formed a cordon that stood firm throughout the whole task. Now, as we approached it, the Iraqi police who manned the checkpoint waved and smiled as we drove past. They had seen the explosion, the Iraqi police car careering around the secondary and the anguish on the faces of every British soldier as they drove past, heads out of the drivers hatch or turret. They seemed so smug, so happy.

For a moment I lost it. 'Get out of the way, you fucking pricks, you fucking wankers, fuck off you fucking cunts.' They could barely hear through the bulletproof glass of the bomb van but knew exactly what I meant as I caught their eyes. I had never felt so angry, so let down and so without hope in my life. Tears poured down my face as they waved at us, taunting, goading. What the fuck were we doing here if even the police wanted us dead?

My will to fight was torn from me. It was not only the reality of the deaths but the agony of the truth. No matter how much blood was spilt in their cause, the people of Al Amarah did not appreciate a single drop of it.

Fitzy and I sat in silence, neither of us able to choose the words that could convey how we felt about the day.

We were soon crossing Sparrowhawk airfield and emerging at the western entrance to camp where each corner, junction and culvert had been cleared by our fellow soldiers. They now stood on top of their Warriors or peered from the open doors of their Snatch vehicle in silent reflection as our convoy rolled past, looking every inch like a funeral procession.

Major Harry Corwell, the second-in-command of the Scots DG Battle Group, stood at the west gate to welcome us back. He had been monitoring the incident from camp but knew little of the detail.

'Kevin ... what happened? What was it?'

'Rich and Lee Ellis are dead.' My eyes filled with tears as I stared at the ground. 'And right now we have nothing to stop it happening again.'

The Adjutant sprang out of his chair and opened the door

to the CO's office as soon as Harry and I approached. Colonel Ben Edwards' office was a large room dominated by a huge table, a map of Maysaan and, tucked away in the right-hand furthest corner, a small desk covered in stacks of files surrounded by empty mugs. The CO nodded slowly as I outlined the day's events, saying little but taking in every detail and for a second closing his eyes, placing his palms together as if in prayer, and taking a single deep breath. For agonizing seconds, or minutes, or longer we sat still as Colonel Ben contemplated his next move.

'It's time for my 'O' Group [briefing meeting]. I shall see you there in a minute.' Harry and I left, closing the door slowly as Colonel Ben remained stationary, for those few moments probably one of the loneliest men on the planet.

That night, as the briefing finished, the CO spoke:

'Today has been a tragedy. We have lost two outstanding men but we must carry on.' He slowly eyed each of the twenty exhausted faces in the room. I wondered if anyone else in that room felt sick at the thought of ever leaving camp again.

'And tomorrow morning,' he continued, 'the first patrol out will be a Snatch patrol,' he paused, 'and I will be sitting in the front of the first Snatch.'

I sat in awe, wishing I was half the man Colonel Ben was. No one else in that room apart from the CO, Harry and I knew exactly how dangerous that decision was. He had taken the most dangerous seat in the least protected vehicle the Battle Group possessed; he was not about to order his soldiers to do something he was not prepared to do himself.

The hubbub of conversation grew quieter as the 'O' group dispersed from the briefing room. I stayed behind; to my right, under a small map of Al Majar Al Kabir was the bench where Rich usually sat. No one had taken his place tonight.

'Are you OK?' The QM had walked past the open door and

seen me sitting inside alone. He had served for nearly thirty years and had seen it all. There was no point in lying, he would see through that in an instant. I looked back, forced a smile and gathered my body armour, helmet and notepad.

'I don't know.'

12. TRAUMA

28 February – 1 March 2006

'Two fatalities, one secondary.'

I had waited my entire career for that phone call; as soon as I heard it I had known that my life would never be the same again. Something had driven me to want to test myself in the toughest way imaginable; was it a desire to prove something to others? To myself? Or was it just the thrill of action that motivated me? Whatever my reasons for wanting the immediate, fast rush of danger, I had certainly never bargained for the slow ache that would remain for so long after the adrenalin had passed.

The task had exposed me to so many sights, so many feelings and such fear that I knew that there would have to be some long-term effects. But I had no idea just how damaging it would be.

Post Traumatic Stress Disorder (PTSD) was mentioned in pre-deployment training and would be discussed again in a mandatory one-hour briefing before I left Al Amarah. But, other than its existence, and that it used to be called Shell Shock, I knew very little about it. I certainly had no idea of how to treat it or just how destructive it could be. It would have been much easier to diagnose and assist others if I had not been reeling from the shock of the day myself.

As I looked around the EOD Ops room that evening, my

team sat silent, locked inside their own minds. Fitzy looked at the floor, Claire sat back in her chair focusing on the ceiling, and AJ repeatedly wound the end of his green rifle sling around his finger before undoing it and starting again. Jay, the bundle of energy who had seemed indefatigable until now, slumped forward holding the brim of his desert hat in both hands. Everyone seemed older, even somehow smaller than they had this morning. In the air around us the smell of the battlefield, of sweat, grime and dried blood brought the ghosts of Lee and Richard into EOD House.

I knew nothing of how to treat trauma other than that it was important to talk. Talk to people with similar experiences, talk to people who could understand, talk to anyone who would listen. Just talk. Unspoken memories would fester in our minds, reappearing later in our lives as violence, nightmares, flashbacks or worse. If we did not talk now, so soon after the event, it would become much harder to do so in the future.

It's said that more soldiers have killed themselves since the Falklands than were killed during it. I had no time whatsoever for any bravado or pretence that we would not be affected by the day's events, and was determined that I would do everything I could to help my team members who, even now, after they had seen me at my weakest, needed and expected me to help. The officer, the ATO, would know what to do; I would lead them through this trauma.

For all my training, all my experience, all the advice I had taken on bomb disposal, I had never asked anyone what happens after the bomb disappears. I could dismantle the most sophisticated devices known to man but had not been given a minute's training on how to cope afterwards.

One by one we discussed our experiences, each of us remembering different versions of the same task, a common experience with very individual elements.

Fitzy spoke of his fears before we had reached the scene and of how the look of shock on my face when I had told them about Rich had shaken his nerve. He had never seen me like that before. I had always sought out danger, always been the one who had led the team forward with confidence and never revealed my dread. As we tore towards Al Amarah, Fitzy had glanced sideways and seen a different person in the passenger's seat, absolutely quiet, contemplating, eyes welling with anger, trepidation and sadness.

As I walked up to the device the first time, Fitzy had been locked in the dark cabin of his ECM van with no idea of the situation outside and with little hope of his ECM kit working at all. He couldn't see or hear the crowd and had no idea whether I was 20 metres or 20 centimetres away from the bomb. The metal cabin even stopped his radio from working, so he sat alone, terrified, and awaiting what we all believed was inevitable: a blast wave that would signal my demise and the start of the battle for anyone who remained. I, naively, had thought that the limited protection from the blast, gunshots, stones and fire that hailed on to his van would have comforted him, but he lacked two vital elements: situational awareness and a belief that his risk was making a difference. His ECM kit worked so infrequently that it was almost useless. Was he risking his life for nothing?

Jay was racked with guilt, believing that negligence on his part had caused me to take the Longest Walk. His voice broke constantly as he described the drive to Al Amarah and the crippling agony of feeling that he had let me down. This wasn't about a corporal letting a captain down; it was about mates, brothers in arms, and he felt he had committed the ultimate sin – failing another soldier. But there was nothing he, or I, could have done to avoid it. We had identified the fault, reported it and tried to fix it ourselves, all to no avail. We were the first team to find the problem and the first to unnecessarily risk our lives because of it; it was just plain bad luck.

His guilt was matched by the helplessness he had felt as, moments after I had told him I had little hope of surviving, I had started to approach the device. As I turned and walked he had felt absolutely powerless and could only watch as I passed out of view and towards what he believed was certain death.

Even Claire could not shake the images of her day from her mind. She was tough, but her photography had burned those awful images of the day into her memory.

AJ seemed distant; he had spent a lot of time behind the van in the ICP and less time at the scene of the explosion. I wondered whether he was subconsciously protecting himself from the images before him at the scene.

The incredible detail recalled by my team was in stark contrast to my own memory. Already it had started to block images of Lee in the Snatch vehicle and Rich covered in the blanket. My subconscious was trying to protect me and was slowly shutting my memory down. I could see so clearly the Para wings on Rich's right arm, a mark of his fitness and soldiering skills, but nothing else. Maybe that was just how I liked to remember him – as a soldier. I could not understand it: the two most overpowering images I had ever seen were locked away in some dark corner of my consciousness and I had little access to them. I suspected then that I was just storing up problems for later but could do nothing about it.

That night, EOD House was visited by Martin, the Padre. He was very well respected by all of us and had a very accurate finger on the pulse of the Battle Group. He enquired about the welfare of my team, what had happened that day and spoke to each of them in turn. This wasn't about religion or offering the support of God: this was a man offering to listen, and that was enough. Finally, after the team had left, he came to me.

'Kevin – how are *you*?' Word of my actions had spread, and Martin knew me well enough to see that I was not the type of person who could just brush off the day's events.

It was the first time that anyone had asked me that, and the first time that I had looked inwards to try and assess how I was feeling. I cried. The two of us sat alone in the EOD Ops room as I told him of my experiences that day, the emotion washing over me as I recounted the horror of seeing Richard's body and the other sights, smells and fears that had stuck in my mind. Martin knew exactly how to listen, gently leading me to other memories with subtle questions.

Later, alone in my room, I sat on the floor and stared at the dull white wall in front of me. Since returning from the battlefield I had tried to eat but could not; the canteen where I had seen the Paras with their television crew this morning was silent, and my appetite was non-existent. Even after showering I could still smell the battlefield on me.

The night of 28 February was long and restless. My heart pounded and my mind raced as I lay still. Martin had left me with some relaxation exercises, which I performed whilst listening to my iPod, but I was wired, high on adrenalin and had no chance of sleep. Flashes of memory brought images of Rich lying alone in the dust, shattered, lifeless – there but not there.

It wasn't just memories that kept me awake that night; an immense feeling of guilt crushed my soul. I had not planned the attack, planted the bomb or rejoiced after the explosion, but I was responsible for training the Battle Group in Counter-IED procedures. Two men had died on my watch. Had my training not been good enough? Was there any more that I could have done?

What I could not understand was how unjust their deaths had been. Paratroopers are the finest infantry soldiers in the

British Army; they are tough, dedicated, professional and absolutely fearless. Rich and Lee were both first-class soldiers and did not deserve to die this way. They had not been beaten by other soldiers, not out-thought, out-fought or out-shot. They had lost their lives cheaply to a cowardly foe who could never match their soldiering skills.

It was not only that they were dead; it was the utter lack of dignity in their loss and the shattering of their identity as soldiers. Rich had been thrown on to the road while Lee remained in his seat, but their possessions – their rifles, bullets, dog tags and body armour – were everywhere, all over the road. It was these visual reminders of my fallen colleagues that would haunt me the most. Even Rich's rifle was shattered. His *rifle*. It was as if the terrorists had designed a bomb to remove any memory of Rich's character – his life as a soldier.

My fury threatened to boil over as I thought of the terrorists laughing and celebrating their victory. Two kills and they had got away without a scratch. At that moment I couldn't settle for their arrest; I wanted them dead. I wanted a Warrior to smash through their walls while men fast-roped down from helicopters overhead. I wanted them to beg for mercy as the red laser streaming from the SA80 found their faces in the dark, to know what it feels like to lose friends as the first shots rang out. It wouldn't change history, but it was what they deserved.

I had arrived an hour after the explosion, but now my mind played tricks. I had spent the task deciphering the sequence of events and now I found myself imagining them as if I had been there. Who had placed the bomb? Why had they targeted the Snatch vehicle? How did they think I would attempt to defuse it? My mind worked overtime trying to understand exactly what happened; I thought of the EFP as it initiated, a fraction of a second later killing Lee and Rich. I had conducted this kind of post-blast investigation so many times before, but had never lost a friend or dwelled so much on the grim details.

For all the conflicting emotions that filled my mind, I fought to keep my experience in perspective. I had it easy: there were other soldiers in the Snatch vehicle with Rich and Lee who would have heard the explosion, felt the blast and seen their friends dead within a matter of seconds. And then they soldiered on.

I remembered my excitement on passing the High Threat course, my disappointment at not being sent to Iraq straight-away, and my desire to see real action while I was here. Fucking hell, I was so naive, so green. I had now seen conflict and had no desire ever to see it again. The derring-do of the ATO who would charge out of camp for the slightest reason had gone forever. I simply did not want to go on another task. I reflected on the theory that courage is a finite resource and that once you have spent it, you can never replace it. I was overdrawn, and felt cold at the thought of ever wearing my bomb suit again.

Then it struck me: it wasn't us here in Al Amarah that would be worst affected by the attack. For the first time in my life I prayed, not for me, not for the Battle Group, but for Lee and Richard's families. How dare I feel sorry for myself? Rich and Lee had wives, Lee had a baby girl.

I could not imagine how they would feel when they opened the door to see an officer in service dress and a padre standing on their step. They might even know the officer; he would remove his hat, his medals and leather belt shining in the sun. Perhaps they would have been to his house, met his family, shared a beer – even shared laughter. Now there would be a completely different look in his eyes. Would he even have to say 'I'm so sorry'?

13. HOLDING ON

1–2 March 2006

As the Lynx circled above me I promised myself that I would try and maintain a stiff upper lip when John, the SAT, landed. He was coming to Al Amarah for a few days to check on the team and, I suspected, report back to the OC on whether we were still fit to operate.

I already knew the answer: we were fucked. *I* was fucked.

The task had changed everything. Twenty-four hours earlier I would have laughed at the thought of prayer, asking God to help the families left behind. Now, with no rational reason for me still having a pulse, I had begun to wonder: how was I still here?

John had lived through the ordeal with us via the only link he had: my infrequent phone calls. Hundreds of miles away, with little idea of the situation on the ground, he couldn't prevent himself from assuming the worst case scenario and dreading the next phone call from Jay. The responsibility on his shoulders had been immense; he had given me the authority to conduct the manual approach. Fingers would have been pointed at him before the smoke had cleared if it had gone wrong. It takes balls to risk your own life, but far bigger balls to risk some else's.

The heli had barely touched down before he emerged from the dust storm, the still-spinning rotors flicking stones all around the landing strip and causing me to shield my face. Once again I felt tears welling in my eyes and shook my head in disgust. I was a captain in the British Army, a soldier for the last seven years, and my team needed me to be strong. No one had ever seen me like this before Red One. This wasn't how soldiers were supposed to act.

'Alright, sir?' He sounded cheery but the question was clearly rhetorical. The heli had by now lifted off but still I protected my eyes. Any excuse not to let him see how red they were. He had the answer to his question before I had taken his bergan and slung it over my shoulder: the ATO Al Amarah was non-operational.

Our short walk back to EOD House was almost completely silent. The endless drone of the many sand-coloured generators sitting outside each building provided welcome relief, a reason for our lack of conversation far easier for two soldiers to accept than admitting the truth; we just did not know what to say. Rounding the path which led past the Thinking Bomb I finally gestured towards the clear bag in John's right hand.

'Better late than never.' Inside the clear plastic bag a factory-fresh ECM power-supply sat in all its vacuum-packed glory.

'Aye. It's amazing how fast a stores system can move when a major general hears of IEDD teams nearly getting wiped out for the sake of a £10 cable.' John had tried as hard as we had to get hold of this piece of kit and had let the general know how close we had come.

I couldn't believe it. Some prick in Basra had decided that my life and the lives of my team were not worth the effort of sending a cable up here until a two star general had kicked his arse.

We stopped briefly at the Thinking Bomb as he delivered his own bombshell. I was to be stood down for twenty-four hours. John would replace me.

The Battle Group had seen the state I was in and demanded that I be given a break. He tried to soften the blow by saying it was just a precaution, that he was looking out for the best interests of the team and that in a day I would be back in command. I protested that he did not know the area, the team or the Battle Group, but all to no avail. The decision was made.

For the second time in twenty-four hours I faced my fears alone. This time there was no bomb, no PIR, just my team who had so often taken incredible risks to protect me. How could I possibly tell them I had been given special treatment while they had to carry on as usual? Leaders lead, they don't take time off while their men crack on.

I could not look them in the eye as I broke the news. They said little but I sensed their disappointment; my only consolation was that it was nothing compared to how bad I felt. Perhaps this was how Jay had felt when he told me of the Wheelbarrow. I left the room before anyone had the chance to react – a selfish act to protect myself from further looks of pity and resentment.

The feeling of guilt at losing Rich and Lee was magnified tenfold as I questioned my actions further. Was there some question over the decisions I had made? Did they think I had unnecessarily risked my team's lives? That would be unforgivable; perhaps they had replaced me while they reflected on whether to sack me altogether – certainly no one from the EOD Group had commended us. Had I fucked up so massively? Should I have just said 'No, I can't do it'?

I had never felt so low in my life. Completing the task is one part of being a bomb disposal operator, but coping after an incident was just as significant; had I failed the test I had waited for all my life?

I had no doubt that I was physically exhausted and needed a rest, but so did the rest of the Battle Group. The twenty-four hours off probably seemed like the right thing to do but it succeeded only in giving me time to dwell on my decisions, replaying each one, questioning my every move.

An outsider for twenty-four hours, I was detached from the rhythm of camp and spent my time perched on the Thinking Bomb as life continued all around me. On the surface, life in the Battle Group appeared normal; Warriors still tore up the ground; Challengers grunted their way around camp and platoons still returned wearily from the town. But we had changed; troops walked less purposefully than before, groups of soldiers lingered longer and spoke less, the strip of road outside EOD House was silent, even as dozens of men walked to the cookhouse.

There was so much to say, but barely a word passed anyone's lips. Forty-eight hours ago the Battle Group was at the peak of its powers, blooded, hungry, and effective. We had lost men before, but never had the Battle Group received such a vicious body blow as that delivered on 28 February.

'You know what I'm looking forward to?'

Padre Martin had appeared at my side and paused for dramatic effect.

'A big fucking beer and some curry. Now move over. There's room for two.'

I laughed; the man of God was just as human as the rest of us.

'I want a *citron pressé*.' For a few precious minutes we sat in silence. I had promised myself a trip to Paris on my return home and could not wait to enjoy a delicious lemon drink on the Champs-Élysées. I imagined myself sitting still, emptying my mind and watching the world go by as the pressure drained away.

'What's going on in there?' He gestured at my head. I looked at my watch: we had probably been sitting together for fifteen minutes and I hadn't said a word. I hardly had the mental space to think about interacting with people; my mind was running overtime just trying to sort out what the hell it had been put through.

'Oh ... God I have no idea. A million things ...' I shook my head. 'I keep replaying the day, questioning every move I made. Why did I choose to manual the device? Surely I could have blown it up with a round from the Warrior? Was I right to take Fitzy with me? Should I have done it on my own?'

Martin nodded. 'Go on.'

'Worst of all, I told Jay before I walked that this was it, that I had no chance of surviving and asked him to pass on messages to my parents and ex-girlfriend. I scared the living shit out of him. But how else were they supposed to know I was thinking of them?' I paused, only for a second, the floodgates were open.

'And I can't remember anything. I can't remember seeing Lee, barely remember seeing Rich and cannot imagine not thinking about this every day for the rest of my life. How the hell do you go back to normal life after that?'

Such was the weight of my emotion and the memories of fear and loss that I could never imagine a time when the thoughts of 28 February would not be lurking somewhere in my mind.

'It's not just me though, Padre. I have seen it in other guys too. A Highlander came by here earlier and told me of how he had walked with me toward the bomb on my first manual, along the road past Rich and Lee, past the shattered Snatch vehicles to the halfway point and had then said "Go on Sir, you're a good guy but I've got to leave you here."'

Martin said nothing. I continued: 'And of course nothing like that happened at all. I walked in front of Fitzy as he drove the ECM van and neither of us remembered anyone else being near us at all.'

I was sure that the Highlander did not believe he was lying; a man like that had nothing to prove to me. He was absolutely certain that it did occur, but it couldn't have. I had all the respect in the world for the man but would never had let him walk with me towards the device. That was my job and mine alone.

'Don't believe for a minute that this doesn't affect everyone.' Martin gestured towards the accommodation to our north.

'Everyone in there, regardless of how many badges, tattoos or ops tours they have under their belt suffers to some extent. I have seen RSMs cry just as often as the youngest soldiers. You know what the difference is?'

I shook my head.

'RSMs look for help; the youngsters bottle it all up.'

Martin looked at his watch; we had run out of time: Rich and Lee's memorial service was due to start. 'And if I don't turn up on time I will really be in the shit.' He laughed aloud as dusk enveloped us.

Patrols were stopped, life in camp slowed, for an hour the connection between Battle Group and Al Amarah was broken as we looked in on ourselves. Operational tours provided little time to grieve and we had to take whatever opportunity we could.

The tall memorial at the northern end of the grassed area outside Battle Group Ops provided the backdrop for the ceremony. Made up of five separate whitewashed stone walls, ranging in height from 1.5 to 3 metres high, which stood behind a tall wooden cross, the memorial was adorned with wreaths and plaques inscribed with the names of the fallen. Maybe its designer knew more about the resilience of the Iraq insurgents than most of the generals and politicians; its walls had sufficient space to take many more plaques.

I recognized many of the names already present on the memorial from news features and friends' war stories: Lieutenant Richard Shearer had been killed by an EFP, Corporal

Simon Miller was one of the Red Caps killed in Al Mak and Lance Corporal Allan Douglas, one of ours, had been shot by a sniper. The simple wreath lying at the foot of the wall had been placed some months earlier and had a single sentence written on a small white card pinned to the centre.

'*We will remember them.*'

The southern and eastern sides of the courtyard were packed with the fighting companies of the Battle Group, the rest of us occupying the western edge nearest Battle Group Ops. The sense of deflation, of frustration, was palpable. The rocketing had jabbed us into exhaustion and set us up for the cruellest of blows on 28 February.

Opposite me, directly across the courtyard, a large gap marked the absence of D Company, The Parachute Regiment. They had felt the losses most keenly of all and were now nowhere to be seen; only a few minutes before the service was due to start we were missing the people who needed to be here most of all.

The faintest whisper began to echo across the camp from the D Company lines, the gentle, almost imperceptible rhythmic thump of boots on the earth. The chatter slowly subsided as more of us heard the crunch of sand underfoot, the unmistakable sound of a body of men marching.

'Dig, dig. Heel, toe, heel, toe.' That voice could only have belonged to Company Sergeant Major Janner, the 6'3" Para who I so often saw at the front of the Para PT as it tore past EOD House.

The drumming of men marching grew louder and more confident as D Company rounded the edge of the memorial wall and silhouetted themselves against the light coloured dust storm they threw up behind.

'Doft, aight, doft, aight, doft, aight.'

Never 'left, right, left, right': the barked instructions keeping each man perfectly in step boomed around the courtyard as the Paras prepared to halt. All eyes were fixed on D Company as they marked time.

'Halt!' Sergeant Major Janner's command still reverberated around the courtyard as the lightning strike of a perfectly timed halt pierced the dusk, every boot striking the floor simultaneously.

'Riiiight … TURN.' Now facing into the courtyard, it was clear that, although their loss had hurt, they would not spend long licking their wounds. With not a hair or thread out of place, they looked as sharp as any battalion on Horse Guards.

The mood of the Battle Group began to lift: fuck it, if they can get over it – if they can soldier on – then so can I.

Initially I stood alone, engrossed in my own thoughts as the sermon was read, but as details of Rich and Lee's life were described by the CO, Rhiannon, the doctor who had done so much to counsel so many others after the attack, appeared next to me and tried to smile through her tears.

The first notes of 'Highland Cathedral' broke us all; tears flowed freely as the Scots DG Pipe Major stood alone in the centre of the courtyard, the notes drifting out into the desert. Rhiannon and I linked arms and for the first time since the task I felt free to be upset, to allow tears to flow and to let the sadness and anger of the day flood out. I was not alone; the finality of our loss had hit home and for the first time we could grieve as a Battle Group.

Tears soon gave way to smiles as Rich's friend Will Davidson, a Highlanders captain, played the theme tune from Rich's favourite film, *The Longest Day*, on the keyboard. At that moment in Basra, Lee and Rich's coffins were being loaded onto an RAF C-17 to begin their journey home.

The Battle Group dispersed and I walked slowly back to

the accommodation with Padre Martin, Rhiannon and Mike Maguire, the Battle Group Engineer. I had never before drunk a drop of alcohol on operations but now, as Martin poured glasses of champagne from a secret stash in his cabin, I could not resist. We sat still, each of us taking in what had happened. Rhiannon broke the silence.

'The first time I met Rich was at a fancy dress party in Germany. People came dressed as nurses, monks, disco queens – but nobody could find Rich. All night people looked for him; lifting up fake beards, removing masks, all to try and find him amongst the revellers. No one had a clue whether he was the guy dressed in the bear costume, the one who had worn a chicken outfit all night or even whether he had turned up at all.'

She paused, sipping champagne for effect.

'Until someone found a man dressed as a Ninja, bodypopping on the dance floor. It was unmistakable – no one else danced like that!'

I told the group of the time Rich had tasked me to an oil tanker full of anti-tank mines in the centre of town. I had to find a way of breaking into the tanker, did not want the locals to see how I did it, and, thinking little of it, I threw a few smoke grenades down to mask my actions. As I carried on with my task, Rich ran in, furious: he had just bought the Iraqi Police brand new cars and now my red smoke had turned them all pink. He loved the Iraqis. There was nothing he would not do for them, even if it meant running through noxious smoke toward a tanker-sized bomb. I laughed aloud as I remembered his hair covered in red smoke as he hopped up and down in anger.

I recalled seeing him every day jogging back from the gym with a huge smile on his face. He was thin, wiry and as fit as anyone in the Battle Group – he wouldn't have it any other way.

Aside from the oil tanker incident, I only ever saw Rich with a huge smile all over his face.

Our glasses clinked together one last time; I was late for a meeting with the Battle Group 2IC and would have to dash.

'To Rich and Lee,' I said, before finishing my glass. I left the group with a heavy heart; I would have loved to have stayed with them a bit longer. I loved the camaraderie of my own team, but it was nice to enjoy some luxury and banter away from EOD House for a while too.

Harry, the Battle Group 21C, met me with a warm smile and directed me to a quieter area of camp where we could talk without interruption. Each Battle Group maintains a 'War Diary' containing the details of major actions, battles and incidents, and he needed my input to flesh out the detail.

We spoke for hours. Harry extracted every single detail I could remember about the day. I told him about receiving the call, moving to the Ops room and stopping the QRF driving through the secondary. We spoke about the Wheelbarrow and how I realized from that point that I would have to manual the device.

Describing the task itself was incredibly difficult, Harry was not at the scene so needed me to draw and detail where all the vehicles were, where Rich and Lee were and how close the crowd had got. Re-living every single detail was hard, but probably cathartic and I appreciated him taking the time to listen. He didn't need all these details. Like John, he was trying to assess how the task had affected me.

He got his answer when I described how before I left the ICP I had told Jay about Beth and my parents.

'My God'. He looked shocked. 'You were that certain.'

'Yep.' I nodded slowly. 'I have no idea why I am alive. There was just no way to beat that bomb.'

My head tipped forward and Harry put his hand on my

shoulder. I was overwhelmed by memories of the day and could not cope with re-living every second of it again.

My route back to EOD House was long. I needed time to empty my mind and wipe away the tears. Physically and emotionally I was a wreck, and would never be the same gung-ho officer I had been before. I only had two weeks of my tour left and had to hope that there would be no repeat of the horrors of that day. I had a team to lead, but wondered whether I would be capable of doing so anymore.

'I hear it was tough out there at Red One.'

Major Alex Brenman was visiting his troops on sentry and startled me as he appeared from the darkness.

He continued: 'It hurts to lose friends. I have lost a dozen or so in my time. But you will get over it. Every time you get a good night's sleep you will wake up feeling stronger. Give it a month or so and you will want to soldier again.'

'That's difficult to believe right now.'

'I know. That's natural, but look, if there is one piece of advice I can give you, don't see a shrink. They all have their own agendas and mess with your mind. Don't waste your time.'

I nodded. This was something I would just have to get through myself. I just had to man up, soldier on and get over it.

As the Lynx carrying John back to Basra disappeared from view, I crossed my fingers and hoped that my last two weeks in Iraq would be quiet. Whatever reserves of courage I had before 28 February had disappeared and the thought of deploying outside the camp brought such intense anxiety that I feared I would not be able to do it at all.

I sought refuge from the demands of the EOD group and intensity of Battle Group operations away from the Thinking Bomb. If I sat there people would see me, stop to talk and constantly discuss 28 February. I was too tired to think and needed to escape. Behind EOD House a large open area of baked clay, scattered rubbish and large grooves where armoured vehicles turned as they drove to the tank park provided a respite from Battle Group life.

A small concrete step linking the house and the clay acted as my perch as I spent hours throwing small pieces of mud at tiny marks on the ground. The generator humming loudly next to me kept others away and shielded me from the sounds of camp which I had once loved and now abhorred. I couldn't hear the thump of a Merlin's rotors without being drawn right back to Red One. However, my step could not protect me from everything.

The phone rang again.

The Battle Group received information on a bomb that had been planted in the centre of Al Amarah, on Route 6. A complex search operation would have to be mounted to clear the area; I would lead with the REST in support and D Company of The Highlanders providing protection. We would sweep around the eastern edge of the town as a bluff and then dart west into the centre, by Red One, before heading south along Route 6 and clearing the length of the road.

The operation would take place in two days and last four or five hours. Throughout that entire time my heart didn't stop pounding. For two days I felt nothing but fear. The Battle Group had received so many of these reports and they always seemed to turn out to be false – why on earth would we waste assets and put so many people at risk for no real gain? I was furious, and let my objection be known to the Battle Group staff who took it for what it was – a plea not to leave camp once again. The threat was credible – we would have to clear it.

'Hey, El Capitano.' Jay and I were walking in front of the bomb van as we turned south at the water tower towards the supposed location of the bomb. We were only 100 metres away from where the crater from 28 February still sat. I nodded to Jay in acknowledgement.

'How are you feeling?' he said, motioning down towards Red One. With the exception of a few taxis and a couple of dozen people, the area was largely clear. Normal life had resumed minutes after my convoy had returned to camp. Life in Al Amarah was like that: a couple of British deaths would barely have raised eyebrows in the rows of barbers and dingy cafes that lined the route south from the water tower.

'I'm OK.' I wasn't and he knew it.

'It's just that you haven't said much since we set out and me and the guys were a bit worr– . . .'

I spun towards him, for a second forgetting my surroundings. 'Jay, why don't you just shut the fuck up? Do your job and let me carry on with mine.' I stood face to face with the guy who had saved my life more times than I could remember and eyeballed him. 'Maybe *you* have been a bit different since that fucking task, maybe we all have. Why do you keep fucking hassling me about it?'

He stood still. The locals stopped to stare and the infantry cordon commander appeared from the top of his Warrior, removed his headset and looked on, almost imperceptibly shaking his head. I knew what that meant; I had overstepped the mark and taken out my own anger on a guy who didn't deserve it, who had held the team together when I needed it the most and who was one of my best friends.

Behind me Fitzy had appeared from the cab of the ECM vehicle and looked at me, then at Jay. I recognized that look; it wasn't anger or pity, just sadness. We had won the battle at Red One but I was showing every sign of losing the war and dragging others with me. Gone was the happy-go-lucky charger who relished the streets. It was obvious to everyone involved that I needed to get the hell out of Al Amarah quickly.

The search that day was fruitless. As was the one we did to the south of Sparrowhawk Airfield the next day and the task to the east of the airfield only two days after that.

A short time before I was due to leave Al Amarah, a psychologist visited camp and even offered me an appointment, but I just wasn't interested. I hadn't made it through four months of high threat bomb disposal to give up at the last minute. There was no way I would let anyone mess with *my* mind, no way I would become part of someone's agenda.

Meanwhile I had begun to self destruct – as a person, as a leader and as an officer. I was one of the most experienced bomb disposal operators in Iraq but I could never imagine walking that longest of walks again. Ever.

14. BACK HOME

14 March 2006

Fitzy and I were lucky to leave Iraq two weeks after Red One.

My replacement, Charlie Yorke, and I had known each other since Sandhurst, served together in Germany and even operated together in Northern Ireland. But now, when he arrived in Al Amarah, he found a stranger. After his return from Iraq, and to fill the gaps in my shattered memory, I asked him to describe his arrival in theatre and his feelings upon reaching Camp Abu Naji.

Kevin and I spoke twice on the phone before I moved to Al Amarah. Even over the crackly field telephone he seemed different: quiet, sullen, humourless and unable to express himself. He wanted me to get to Al Amarah as soon as possible and got really agitated when a training package meant I would spend two extra days in Shaiba Logistics Base before flying up there.

One thing he said sounded very ominous, 'It is probably best that you take over duty as soon as you get here, Charlie.' I had no idea why, and he did not wish to discuss it further, but it was clear that he wanted to get out ASAP. That suited me fine. It is difficult to have a predecessor hanging around for too long when you take over a team; you need to make a clean break and do things your own way.

It was clear from his demeanour that Kevin and his team had been affected by the task on 28 February but no one in the EOD Group seemed willing to brief me on exactly what had happened. 'Kevin will tell you all about it,' was as much as I knew as I boarded the plane to Al Amarah. The EOD Group were so distant, geographically and mentally, from Camp Abu Naji that they never fully understood the effect of 28 February on the IEDD team. They knew it was a big task and that they had overcome huge difficulties, horrific sights and great odds to succeed, but had no idea that the team had been shattered as a result of it.

Within five minutes of landing at Sparrowhawk Airfield we were rumbling toward Camp Abu Naji in a convoy of Saxon vehicles, and it was not long before the low sand berm which surrounded Camp Abu Naji loomed into view. Any sense of the town outside of the wire disappeared as we entered the gates and a new world emerged, one where the roar of armoured vehicles was constant and people wore tired faces, dulled by constant fear.

I was struck by how much the place and the people smelled; the air was filthy with smoke and it seemed as if no one had washed for weeks. The whole place was the same shade of yellow and everything seemed much more basic than it had been in Shaiba. Back there the engineer unit where the EOD Group was based often finished work at 5pm and retired to the Pizza Hut or milkshake bar; here they battened down the hatches and readied themselves for the nightly barrage. It was the inevitability of the attacks that seemed most gruelling. They went to sleep each night knowing that they would be rocked from their camp cots by a blast wave, but they had little chance of stopping it.

All new arrivals to Al Amarah attended a security brief before going to their units. Held in the Battle Group briefing room, the walls were covered with pictures of weaponry, maps of local areas and posters describing telltale signs of IEDs. A corporal from the Battle Group Intelligence cell briefed on recent casualties the Battle Group had taken, the many contacts that patrols had and the constant threat of IDF. He seemed tired but left us in no doubt this was not Shaiba Logistic Base; this was war.

Within minutes of arriving at EOD House I could see that the IEDD team were fucked; they were non-operational. Although still in post I had no doubt that Kevin was no longer able to operate effectively, and was a shell of the man I had known since Sandhurst. It seemed as if his personality had evaporated; he had collapsed in on himself and it was clear that physically he was a wreck. He seemed smaller, weaker and much nervier than I had ever seen him before. The ATO is the heart, soul and brain of an IEDD team and this team was screwed.

Jay had lost little of his enthusiasm and greeted me with an 'Alright kidda' but even he seemed quieter, more distant. We had both served in 921 EOD Squadron in Germany and his reputation was first class. Jay still had two months to push and I was concerned: how could he possibly keep going after what he had been through?

Although also a member of 921 EOD Squadron, I knew little of Fitzy but it soon became apparent that he too was desperate to leave. Thankfully his replacement had arrived on the same flight as me and he also took over as soon as he could. Fitzy was extremely quiet and spent nearly as much time sat on the Thinking Bomb as Kevin, gazing silently at passers-by.

The first night saw my first taste of the 220 rockets that would be launched at us during my tour. Tired figures emerged from their beds and dragged on body armour and helmets in a well-rehearsed routine.

This clearly happened a lot.

Shattered men grumbled that the enemy liked to attack us in the early hours of the morning; even if they missed they knew we would all get up, lose sleep and be less able to operate the next day.

Only four months previously I had replaced Kevin as ATO Londonderry, a fantastic time where we had toured the Creggan and the Bogside in PSNI cars seeing the houses and hangouts of local players, and the scenes of recent IEDD tasks. At night we sipped coke in the police bar and talked about every aspect of the IED threat in the city. By the time he left, Kevin had imparted every useful nugget of information he could and I was ready to operate immediately.

This was quite the opposite. I fought through the three-day hand-over and although he was clearly trying, Kevin had nothing left to give. He had completed three tasks outside the wire after 28 February and each one had further decimated any reserves of courage he may have once had. Aside from the Thinking Bomb he spent much time sitting still in the EOD Ops room where his makeshift bed had been made after he vacated the shower room ready for my arrival. He also sat on the step at the back of EOD House. He would sit quietly, saying little and seemed trapped in his own mind.

Whatever the state of the IEDD team, the Battle Group thought of them as heroes. It turned out that the Battle Group 21C, Harry, had ordered the Joint Force EOD Group to replace Kevin for twenty-four hours. I wished it had been longer but thanked Harry for looking after Kevin. Unlike the EOD Group, I think he and the rest of the Battle Group senior officers knew that their IEDD capability had been severely damaged. They understood because they knew exactly what had happened on 28 February and had shared the grief of losing two soldiers.

I had arrived part way through the six-month tour of the Scots DGs and knew I was joining a seasoned Battle Group, but even this group of men and women who had seen and achieved so much over the last four months looked tired. A combination of the isolation of Al Amarah and the constant rockets had worn them down, and they had felt the loss of their men even more keenly because of it.

On occasion Kevin would speak about 28 February. I listened, but was not keen to hear the grim detail. I was only interested in the IED technology involved and how we might combat it. I felt sure that we would have enough blood, fear and combat to deal with ourselves.

It was clear that the combination of seventy-seven rocket attacks and 28 February had severely damaged Kevin and the team. As I dropped them off at the Saxons on their way home, I was left in no doubt of the enormity of the task ahead of me.

On 14 March 2006, Fitzy and I sat in the dust by the Saxon vehicles that would whisk us to the C-130 and out of Al Amarah. This dusty road held so many powerful memories for me: the impact mark of the rocket that nearly took my head off was only 30 metres away; the spot where I had first learned that Rich had died was to my left; the holding area where Jay had told me about the Wheelbarrow, yards to my front; and the gate from which our convoy had rolled out of camp, none of us sure whether we would ever roll back in again, was only 20 metres to my right.

Sitting on top of my bergan I could just see the helipad where four months earlier I had arrived so full of excitement and anticipation. I had relished the opportunity to find war, to fight and test myself, but now felt sick at the thought of returning to this place, wearing a bomb suit or ever taking the Longest Walk again. I had barely managed to operate at all in the last two weeks and had needed more and more support from my team to do the simplest, most trivial of tasks such as completing my daily report to the EOD group. I was broken.

Thousands of other soldiers had sat under these trees at the start of their journey home. We were the lucky ones: many men had been carried directly to Basra by heli or in an ambulance to the C-130 – injured, maimed or dead.

We had left the team only twenty minutes ago and were now less than an hour from leaving camp for good. Jay, Claire and AJ remained with Charlie and would be loaded with more stress and more tasks. I had no idea how they would cope, especially Jay, who had felt the trauma of 28 February more keenly than the others and who still had longest left to push. He had refused to feel sorry for himself and soldiered on, but I wondered whether he had anything left to give at all.

As we sat in the stifling heat we were slowly joined by another forty men and women, some going home for good but the majority due to return after two weeks R&R. I was lucky – no R&R, no brief glimpse of normality before being dragged back to war. I just had to arrive, do my time and leave. How could anyone ever tear themselves away from their family and board the plane back to Iraq in the full knowledge of what lay in store for them?

I could not imagine a time when memories of Rich, Lee and the fear of death would not be at the forefront of my mind. I had asked friends in the Battle Group whether there was any way back to normality and to happiness after such an event. Of course no one knew, and that terrified me beyond belief.

A figure emerged from the other side of the road, Battle Group HQ, as we waited to go home. Unusually, he was on his own and paid little attention to the soldiers rapidly pulling hands out of pockets and avoiding eye contact as they loitered in the courtyard where only a fortnight ago we had wept for Rich and Lee. The RSM, WO1 Cammie Gray, approached, his eyes fixed on Fitzy and me. He looked deadly serious. I hoped I hadn't fucked up and quickly ensured that *my* hands were out of my pockets too.

'Sa!' he barked. I rose quickly from my feet and walked towards him. No one sat down while the RSM stood.

'I'd heard you had had enough of us and were getting the fuck out of here!'

I smiled and took the bait. 'It's just the food, RSM. Me and

Fitzy have both had enough of goat curry.' A few silent seconds passed before the RSM spoke again.

'I just wanted to see you before you both left. What you did on that day was . . .' We fell quiet for another second. 'You and the boys did fucking well; you made us very proud of you all.' I looked at the ground, unable to respond, as the wind took more dust from the road and deposited it over the Saxons that were parked nearby. Around us the hubbub of conversation from our fellow passengers allowed our conversation the privacy it required.

'I still cannot believe it; I keep trying to understand how we could have stopped it . . .'

The RSM stopped me in my tracks. 'Sa.' He fixed me with eyes that had aged years in the last two weeks. 'Don't go down that route; don't let your mind play those games.'

I nodded; the RSM had been on the ground that day and was battling the same demons – demons he had no doubt battled many times before. I wondered how often a man of his experience had seen such terror. Men aged rapidly in the Army: hard work, stress and the effects of life outdoors conspire to create craggy faces, but the fire still raged in their eyes. Today the RSM's eyes were tired. He was due to retire from the Army soon and had, I suspected, seen death far too often.

'Thank you, RSM,' I said, 'and good luck. I just hope the Battle Group gets through the rest of the tour safely.' Even as the words left my lips I knew it was a hopeless ideal. For the first time in four months I caught a glimpse of Cammie Gray the man, rather than the RSM. He stared at the floor for a second, took off his immaculate RSDG beret and ruffled his hair.

'Aye, sir,' the RSM nodded. 'Me too.' We both paused, an unspoken truth that the Battle Group would almost certainly face more challenges just as tough as those on 28 February. With that he turned to Fitzy.

'And don't think I don't know exactly what you did on that day either, young man. I'm proud o' the both o' you.' Fitzy, the scourge of RSMs everywhere with his long sideburns, hands permanently thrust into pockets and ragged uniform, stood bolt upright and shook the RSM's hand.

We both watched as the senior soldier in the Battle Group turned and walked back to his office, his mind already focused on bringing his men back up to their fighting best. Fitzy and I stood for a further minute. The RSM, known as 'Tara' (God) in Scottish Regiments, was a legend in the Battle Group, equally feared and respected by everybody. Words from a man like that carry real weight. As he disappeared from view, I was reassured: even the hardest men could be affected by Iraq.

Before we left, people of all ranks from private to major, some of whom I had never met before, came to say goodbye. Hands were shaken, memories of the day exchanged and embarrassing praise given to my team. Most time was spent in the uncomfortable pauses between memories, time when the images of the day overwhelmed us and we couldn't bring ourselves to speak. As each person left Fitzy and me, as they walked back to their office, Warrior or just into the far corners of camp, the agony of leaving such amazing men and women behind choked me. I was leaving the fight as they battled on.

As the Saxon engines roared into life and the NCO in charge of movements began calling a nominal roll, I realized that I would not miss Al Amarah at all. But Camp Abu Naji, the Scots DG Battle Group and my team had been my world for the last four months and I knew then that I would miss them dreadfully.

The bond that develops between people in adversity is unique: soldiers and officers that I did not know only four months ago had become friends like no other. We had hidden behind the same vehicles as shots rained down on us, laughed together as we discussed the ridiculousness of life in a conflict zone, and cried together when we attended the memorial for Rich and Lee. We had shared a lifetime of emotion in such a short time and now, as I jumped into the back of the Saxon, I knew that I would never share that closeness with them again. The minute you leave camp, conflict or war, that incredible relationship begins to unwind, lives diverge and memories fade.

Peering out of the thick glass as the Saxon door slammed shut, I saw the camp gates for the last time. Out of focus, through the scratched blue tinge of the armoured glass, it could have been a scene from a 1920s movie. And then we drove around the corner and on to the bumpy tarmac road, torn apart by the heavy armour turning and gouging its way into town.

Opposite me was WO1 Joe Lloyd, the REME ASM who had been with me on 28 February. He was leaving on R&R and would have to return to camp two weeks later. It was Joe who had led his men, dodged bullets and recovered the vehicles on the day, that allowed me to determine exactly what had happened to Rich and Lee. He looked exhausted and drawn, and I recognized the distant look in his eyes as the one I and my team had worn since that day. I had not known Joe before this tour but we had got on very well and I respected him hugely. We sat in silence, with Fitzy and half a dozen other soldiers crammed in beside us. I was transfixed by the scene through the window when a friendly kick to the boot brought me back inside the Saxon.

'What fascinates me,' Joe leaned forward, 'is that when that EFP detonated, it created a big metal slug, right?' I nodded. 'Then that slug ended up somewhere. Out there, on the ground, in the middle of the desert or jammed into the side of some building is the thing that went right through the Landrover.'

I nodded. He was absolutely right. One day that slug would be found by someone with no idea of its importance. It would probably be picked up, held close to someone's eye and then discarded as just another piece of street litter.

Each person seemed to focus on different parts of the event. Some, like me, could not think of it without focusing on images of our dead friends. Some remembered the sounds of the crowd and gunfire above all else and some, like Joe, thought about the physical aspects of the attack. The same event, seen through different eyes and processed through different brains, was remembered in a myriad of textures and colours.

Too soon the Saxons screeched to a halt and rear doors were flung open. Before me, a C-130 Hercules aircraft sat only 50 metres away, propellers spinning wildly and kicking up dust all around us. The RAF fire detachment had lined the route between the Saxons and C-130 and were screaming at us to 'MOVEMOVEMOVE!' They motioned violently towards the plane and around me soldiers jogged forward. I wasn't about to run out of Al Amarah and looked each fireman in the eye as I walked past. The plane wasn't going anywhere, we were being protected by a squadron of tanks on the perimeter of the airfield and I had been through too much to run away from this place. Only two steps behind me, Fitzy was in no mood to run anywhere, either.

On board, Fitzy and I looked at each other, half smiled and slumped back into the red netting chairs that ran along the side and through the middle of the plane as we sped down the runway and took off. The journey home was not short – we would stop in Basra and Qatar on our way back to Germany – but as our eyes closed we relaxed and began to try to comprehend that our war was over.

Below us the Battle Group had moved on and was preparing for more patrols, guarding against rocket attack and desperately trying to win the peace in Al Amarah. Armoured convoys waited at the front gate, helicopters slowly descended before unloading cargoes, and soldiers in PT kit ran along the dusty track around camp clutching bottles of water. As Charlie and the team practised rapid drills behind EOD House, the Thinking Bomb was left vacant and the mini twisters went unwatched for a few hours.

Although brief, our stop in Basra Air Station (BAS) to refuel was a window into some soldiers' experience of Iraq. Troops based in Basra would wear the same medal as us, have the same operational tour marked on their records and celebrate as much as we would when they returned home. But we were different. We had been at war for four months and found this new environment, with its unusual smells, rules and relative safety, as foreign as it found us.

To the movements staff who watched us disembark from our C-130, we must have seemed alien to the routine and normality of BAS. The film of dust coating us, our unkempt hair and our scruffy uniforms with shirts hanging out, and desert hats in place of berets, marked us out as different. Inside the terminal, the smell of clean was everywhere; clean people, clean buildings, clean clothes. Grinning, hair-gel-wearing RAF check-in staff rummaged through our bergans searching for contraband as fragrant RAF Regiment gunners flitted around with their shiny bandoliers, decorative grenades and pizza boxes.

BAS could have been Luton Airport. Signs sellotaped to walls indicated the location of the local first aider. Staff shift patterns were marked on calendars, and we were briefed that no large cans of deodorant, carbon paper or nail scissors should be taken on to the plane. Long emptied Starbucks cups attracted flies behind the check-in desk, fresh newspapers were stacked in neat unread piles and countless air-conditioning units buzzed in the background. Returning to civilization was as depressing as landing in Al Amarah had been exciting; I sat still, taking in our new set of priorities.

During our stopover in Qatar, Fitzy and I found ourselves with no desire to join in the celebrations and laughter of the main body of passengers who swilled cans of coke, ate sandwiches and swapped war stories as they waited in the air-conditioned tent that served as the departure lounge for the onward journey to Germany.

Outside the tent, away from the commotion, sitting on two rickety chairs with our feet up on the red and white plastic bollards which penned us in, we sat staring at the clear sky, incredibly bright stars and took in the familiar smells of the desert.

We sat still, alone, and gazed up as the dim lights of aircraft passing overhead darted like shooting stars across the sky. Although the smell of sand was ever present, the air was clean and tinged only slightly by the aviation fuel powering the planes along the runway and into the darkness. It was possible to feel the stresses of Iraq lifting off us as we stared upwards at the clear sky. I wished that Jay was with us and tried to imagine what the team would be doing without us.

Fitzy took a sip from his water bottle and passed it to me. We sat in blissful relaxation, knowing that as soon as we arrived in Germany we would never be as close as we were at that moment, that we had shared the toughest of experiences, and that we had been incredibly lucky to get out alive.

The charter that would take us home had just delivered the latest arrivals to theatre who now milled excitedly in the area behind us. A few troops came to share a cigarette only a metre away from us and could see the kit that Fitzy and I had stacked next to us. Filthy and bloodied body armour, combat helmets with torn covers and blood group stencilled on the back, oil stained daysacks with straps taped up to optimum length.

'That bad is it?!' One of them joked.

We couldn't say anything; we didn't want to scare anyone but could not manage to joke about it either. We sat in silence as the smokers moved away.

From the opposite side of the airfield huge C-17 Globemaster and C – 5 Galaxy aircraft roared along the runway and dragged themselves into the air. Soon, a Monarch airlines plane lumbered into view and we found ourselves back amongst the crowd as we boarded the plane. Officers sat at the front, NCOs at the back and as Fitzy and I separated, a lump in my throat told me that I would dearly miss the relationship I had with my team. Never again in my life would I enjoy such a close-knit, dedicated, selfless group as the one I was a part of in Al Amarah.

Fitzy and I left Al Amarah at 2pm on 14 March 2006 and arrived back to real life in Germany less than twenty-four hours later. As the baggage carousel jolted loudly into action I hit the deck. I had spent four months learning that loud noises were lethal and it would take some time to adapt to real life. I wasn't the only one, a mixture of embarrassment and relief creeping over our faces as we admired the floor.

As we walked from the terminal at Hanover airport, the roads were thick with snow, mothers pushed babies around in prams and flashing neon boards advertised DVD shops, Greek restaurants and cinemas. New cars prowled silently up the road, building sites stood next to recently erected glass-fronted offices, and fat dogs strained at leashes held by young women talking into mobile phones. The air was clear, crisp and cold. This was another world.

We said little as our driver sped us back to Bielefeld and the HQ of 921 EOD Squadron. There was too much to take in, too many colours, too many people, too many new sounds. The brightness of advertising boards and the smell of clean people, aftershave and perfumes seemed overpowering. Senses that had been dulled by the yellowness of Al Amarah and the constant smell of burning that hung in the air, overloaded quickly as my new reality appeared in the windscreen and my mind struggled with the transition from war to real life.

I felt out of place. Physically we looked different; we were tanned, tired and had eyes that showed only the memories of fear. As I looked at young German families enjoying their day, and even at other soldiers as we drove into camp, I realized we *were* different. We had changed as the world stayed the same.

Although I couldn't wait to see my friends and colleagues, I wondered whether they could possibly understand what had happened to us. After all, the vast majority of people would have no frame of reference through which to understand our experiences. How do you tell someone of the terror of waiting for rockets to land, or the horror of walking to your death? And without that understanding, why would they care?

Mick Ireland, the Squadron 2IC, greeted Fitzy and me back to the squadron. Mick, a good friend, sat me down and looking at me through the lens of experience, could see the distress in my face. He explained that the OC of the Joint Force EOD Group had sent a letter to the Squadron explaining the events of 28 February, the trouble I had had coping with it afterwards and that I could expect to suffer some level of mental trauma in the future.

'It was tough, wasn't it?' Mick offered me a glass of port from the ever-present decanter which sat on a small round table next to a huge cut-out of Homer Simpson, a relic from a recent squadron party.

I nodded, dropped my head and looked back up.

'Yep.'

My eyes closed as thoughts of the day pushed to the front of my mind. I was so exhausted, so drained and determined to think about anything other than Iraq. The detail of what happened could wait for now.

'Yep, it was tough. Cheers.' Full glasses, once raised, were quickly emptied and refilled.

One more car journey and three hours later I was back in my room in the Officers' Mess in Bruggen, before having lunch with friends who knew nothing of my actions, little of Iraq and had almost no interest in either. I was lost. The brutal transformation from warrior to nobody was complete less than a day after Cammie Gray had bid us farewell.

Yesterday I had lain shaking in my bed as rockets detonated around us, throwing my body armour on and screaming at others to do the same, as sirens wailed and helicopters took off to search for firing points. Today the internal politics of the Mess was the hottest topic, as gossip was passed on about nocturnal activities after a party the night before.

I relaxed in the opulence of the mess and thought of my friends in Iraq. It would be mid afternoon in Al Amarah. I could sense the rhythm of camp at this time of day: patrols would begin to return to camp before being briefed on arrest operations that evening. OCs and Ops Officers would be planning the following day's activities and the gym would be full as paratroopers exercised to loud dance music, urging each other to lift more weight one more time and chastising those that did not dare to try.

The umbilical cord of common experience had been cut when Fitzy and I had waved goodbye in Bielefeld. Regiments tend to deploy and return en masse and to some extent this can help with decompression and coming to terms with traumatic events. Long nights are spent talking and swilling beer, when damaging memories are brought into the open, discussed and laid to rest amongst friends who could be trusted with the most private thoughts and fears. But I was now alone.

I had been as desperate to leave Iraq, to protect my mind from the relentless blitz of rockets and bombs, as I had been to deploy there and live the dream I had held since my visit to ATO Londonderry.

Somehow I had survived four months as a bomb disposal operator in the toughest town in Iraq. That night should have been one of celebration and relief, beer and laughter, but as I sat on my bergan and looked around my empty room I knew that my battle was far from over.

My body armour clattered into the drawer as, for the first time in months, my life would not depend on it being within arm's reach. My combat trousers would have followed it shortly after, but I had seen something in the pocket and unfolded it to see that it was my A3 map of Al Amarah. For four months I had kept it by my side. It was covered in the blur of a hundred grid references, device descriptions and diagrams. Now it had one more addition, in thick blue pen:

'*Sir, when the time to stand up and be counted arrived, you passed with flying colours. Tam Russell, Sgt Major D Coy.*'

15. DIGGING IN

March 2006

He hardly knew what hit him as I launched myself towards him.

'What the fuck do you know? How much fucking time have you spent there?'

He said nothing, his eyes wide with fear. I was eye-to-eye with Captain Adrian Rosser, a new member of the mess, as onlookers watched in shock. His crime had been to spend thirty minutes criticizing the mission in Iraq and I had snapped, in what was to become a familiar pattern.

Adrian had seen the *News of the World* footage of troops allegedly attacking Iraqi civilians and had heard rumours of Iraqi insurgents being captured and killed by the PWRR Battle Group on Op Telic 4. Al Amarah, he had said, had been a disaster from start to finish and was a waste of time, money and lives. He had barely had time to react as I slammed my glass down and grabbed him by the collar.

'How fucking dare you open your mouth when there are soldiers out there right now?' Arms began to separate us as I continued: 'You're a fucking coward; you go out there and then come back and see if you talk like that again, you spineless prick.' I could not believe that an Army officer, especially one who had never been to Iraq, would be so insensitive as to talk about situations and soldiers he knew nothing about.

I had tried to ignore him as he began his diatribe, to control the irritation that I had felt so many times since coming home. He was ignorant, immature, trying to make a name for himself in the mess and had only just come from his first tour as a Signals Troop Commander in York. I had never hit, or been hit by anyone in my life but as he spoke a hot, overwhelming anger had risen inside me and caused me to explode in fury.

It was the first time I had ever lashed out. That night, as I sat in the darkness of my room, I couldn't stop crying. What was happening to me? I had only been back a few days and my mind was starting to disintegrate. The confident, outgoing Kevin that had left for Iraq only four months before was forgotten as I ricocheted from argument to argument, irritation to anger, fury to violence.

My ability to make friends and build relationships had been replaced with varying degrees of exasperation at the lives of those around me. As they whinged about long days in Germany, soldiers were fighting in Iraq; each increasingly banal conversation on mess politics gnawed at me. There was a war on and these people didn't seem to give a shit.

My infuriation served only to increase the feeling of isolation I felt on returning from theatre. When I needed support the most, I spent most of my time driving people away.

I could barely open my mouth without causing offence or upsetting someone. It was so hard to communicate even with fellow officers whom I had known for years if they had not been through similar experiences to me. We were speaking different languages.

It didn't help that my sole subject of conversation was Iraq. I had initially thought that I could keep this problem to myself, that no one else need know, but any time a chance to speak about 28 February arose, I took it. I could not resist the opportunity to turn light-hearted conversations to serious ones, to talk endlessly about the war, British soldiers and my tour.

Whilst in Iraq I had barely recognized the insomnia, anger and nightmares as possible signs of PTSD. It was much easier to see symptoms in others, especially my own team. If, after being in a war-fighting Battle Group for four months, you appeared to be even more messed up than everyone else, you knew you had serious problems.

Back in Germany it was far more difficult to feel the effects of my ordeal as they crept up on me. I had no perspective, nothing and no one against which to measure how quickly I was being consumed by the trauma of what had happened, only the knowledge that I had changed. The episode with Adrian had confirmed that beyond doubt.

For a week after returning from theatre I 'decompressed' in work, a formal mechanism undertaken Army-wide to try to ease the strain of returning from conflict and to slow the transition from warrior to husband, father and friend.

Too many people had been thrust straight into family life less than a day after leaving the battlefield, and had been cut off from the support system of their regiment and their friends. They found it impossible to understand their partners' lives, worries and problems, which seemed so insignificant compared to the battle for survival that they had left behind. Their partners could barely comprehend the danger and horror of operations, and wondered why their loved one had a much shorter temper than before, why they wanted to spend so much time with their fellow soldiers and why they couldn't understand that it had not been easy for those at home, either. Decompression was a first step toward accepting that it was impossible to adjust so quickly.

In the mess, my fellow officers knew I was decompressing and kept their distance, perhaps hoping that my irrational behaviour would be short lived. For the first few days after returning from Iraq I had spent most of my time alone, locked in my room, inside my own mind and had given little evidence of my pain. All that had changed when they saw me fly across the bar to grab Adrian.

My room became both my jail and my sanctuary. I needed to be alone to avoid the anger that I had inflicted on Adrian. Decompression helped, but the 8am to 4pm lifestyle of my bomb disposal troop was still in stark contrast to the long days in Al Amarah, as though a handbrake had been applied to my life. Less than three weeks had passed since Red One and my life had changed beyond belief; the adrenalin of operational tasks had been replaced by the routine of meetings, annual personnel reports and bomb disposal training. I had returned to earth with a bump. Life had changed, and although my mind had yet to escape the blood-soaked streets of Al Amarah, I now had to switch, almost immediately, to who I was before. I relished the opportunity to relax for the first time in nearly a year, but found that every moment alone was too much time inside my own head.

My feet had barely touched the ground between completing the High Threat IEDD course in mid 2005, my tour in Londonderry and then my time in Al Amarah. I had never thought about what would come after Iraq, only that I needed to get there at all costs. Throughout the last year, work had been my sole focus, any remnants of social life were long forgotten and my continued absences from the mess in Germany had frequently caused other 'livers in' to ask whether I was new. I had been there for two years.

Worse than that, I hadn't seen many of my college friends for years, could barely remember the names of the people I went to school with and knew hardly anyone outside the Army. It wasn't just the last ten months that had been the problem: I had thought of nothing but the Army since I was 16, and it showed.

I looked around my room in the mess and saw little apart from piles of work, books on military history and pictures of my various operational tours, courses and exercises. I had always thought this level of commitment was necessary for someone who wants to achieve so much in their professional life. But I wasn't fooling anyone. I had friends who were better officers than I, who were more successful and who managed to have a real life too. There really is more to life than bomb disposal. I had lived my dream, achieved exactly what I had set out to do and was now absolutely spent.

I slumped into the sofa left by my predecessor, leaned over to pull a can of coke from the fridge, a gift from sympathetic mess staff, and stared at the TV which my parents had bought me years ago. How had I got myself into a position where after the toughest four months of my life, when I needed it the most, I had no one at my side to enjoy life with?

Most people on my flight home had someone waiting for them at Hanover airport. I walked through the hugging masses conspicuous in my singleness and swallowed a very hard dose of reality. Why was I so happy to sacrifice everything else in my life just to feel the buzz of danger?

This obsession with passing courses and operational deployments had cost me dearly; I hadn't had a day off in a year, had lost my girlfriend and feared that I was only beginning to pay a much higher price.

My flash of anger may have alerted the mess to some of the problems I was experiencing, but this was only the most visible of the many symptoms that had overtaken my life since coming home.

I had not slept more than a few hours a night as I relived the events of 28 February. Memories brought adrenalin, more hours awake and even greater time to explore my mind. My heart pounded to the same beat as it had in Iraq and my muscles tensed as I replayed the sound of rockets exploding nearby, alarms wailing and the terror etched into a soldier's face as bullets cracked over his head. I had been overwhelmed by the images I had seen and the emotions I had felt, and was now subconsciously trying to understand everything that had occurred.

To escape the loneliness of insomnia, I watched TV into the early hours and found that my emotional link to images of soldiers in distress, forged during Sandhurst while watching videos of Bosnia and Northern Ireland, had increased tenfold.

Any image on TV, film or at the cinema of UK or US soldiers dying, injured or scared dragged me to despair. It mattered little whether the images were fiction or news footage, the effect was the same. I had seen those scared eyes before, on the faces of sergeant-majors, paratroopers and my own team, and it hurt to see them again.

Sleepless nights and restless days conspired with eight months of operational activity to bring me to the brink of physical exhaustion. Sunrise brought welcome respite from my thoughts; but I could achieve little. I walked around, zombie-like, with no idea how I would escape from this cycle of fatigue.

The mirror told me I looked exactly as I felt: thin, aged, weary and unhappy. As I looked at my reflection I saw no hope in my eyes, just dark, lifeless ponds where there used to be fire and energy.

It wasn't just sleeplessness that began to affect my life. The conflict had become intensely personal; my desire to be back with my team, to understand what they were going through and to reconnect to the Battle Group life-support system caused me to obsessively follow every newspaper article, TV report or internet blog on Al Amarah. It was the cruellest contradiction; as I took in the images of burning Snatch vehicles or downed Lynx helicopters in Basra, I would be both addicted and appalled by what I saw. I needed my fix of news but could barely stand to hear it at all.

The pile of desert camouflage uniform in the middle of my room had remained untouched for days. I had expected never to want to see it again but now longed to be back with the team, back in Iraq, back on the Thinking Bomb, while also dreading the nightmares that took me back there every night.

Any number of triggers could send me right back to the scene in Iraq. Any image of a Snatch vehicle would hold me in a trance as I imagined the same vehicle mangled, with holes through the doors and windows smashed. The smell of Land-rovers was also incredibly difficult to bear. It had hung in the air as I had spoken to Tam Russell and McNeil and was seared into my memory thereafter. A distinctive military smell, it now sickened me.

Lying under my mosquito net during the fortnight before I left, I had listened to entire albums by Joni Mitchell, Eva Cassidy and Norah Jones. The slow, relaxing music I had used in Iraq to lower my heart rate, calm my nerves and let me steal a few hours sleep now had the opposite effect. The same artists, songs and memories were off limits, raising my heart rate and causing me to revisit Red One and my friends once more.

I was a spectator to my own emotions as the temper that I and the rest of the mess had already seen got even worse, flaring for the most innocuous reasons. Trivial matters such as soldiers arriving for meetings a few minutes late, the endless stream of paperwork that poured in from Regimental HQ or the ignorance of my fellow officers of what was happening in Iraq, caused my blood to boil. Irrational anger, out of all proportion to the problem at hand, welled up inside me and erupted at will.

When I accepted my fate on 28 February and walked towards certain death, I understood what it was to die, to have no hope of ever seeing my family again. I think a part of me believed I should have died on that day and was constantly trying to amend a historical aberration.

The combination of guilt and my own acceptance of death set me on a horrendously self-destructive cycle. What if I could return to Iraq, try and save more lives? Would that make up for the loss of Rich and Lee? And if I died, would it matter? Wasn't every breath I took now just a pure fluke anyway?

Combat in its own right did not appeal to me, but the thought of seeing action and making a difference, doing what I could to save soldiers' lives, would not leave me. I tried to snap out of it, to accept that I was just incredibly lucky and that I should not tempt fate ever again, but the feeling of unfinished business would not release its stranglehold.

But what if I did return, save lives and make it out alive? Would I then have to return again? Would I just keep going until they got me? Would that finally give me the perspective I needed on life? Was part of my mind determined to keep pushing me until I was killed?

My survival had even caused me to question my most fundamental beliefs. I had been force-fed God each morning at college and resented every second of it. The irony of enforced religion at a technical college was not lost on me as we were herded into the small chapel. I had never seen any evidence of God, was studying science A-levels and could not reconcile my belief in atoms, evolution and logic with ideas of creation and the Bible. Science was real; it was predictable and repeatable. Everything had a cause.

But 28 February had changed that. My mission to understand how I had survived had proved fruitless. I had collected evidence that proved the presence of a radio-control switch, PIR switch and EFP, and no further evidence was needed of the sniper whose rounds ricocheted off the Warrior armour packs far too frequently. I knew all too well my lack of ECM protection, that my success against any PIR was down to no more than an educated guess and that the sniper could have taken me out with a single squeeze of his trigger.

Perhaps a battery, connection or wire could have been faulty? Maybe the sniper assumed I would die at the device anyway? It all seemed so unlikely: the enemy were so much better than that. Devices were made to high standard in Iran, were easy to assemble and could even be tested before they were placed. Furthermore, the first device *had* worked. If the bomber was incapable of manufacturing a bomb, surely both would have failed?

So why did I survive? Was there maybe some other force at work? I contemplated the idea that a god, a something, had let me survive, and simultaneously chastised myself for being so arrogant. If a god did exist, why on earth would he care about me as I sweated toward the device on Red One?

But every few weeks I pulled my Gideon's bible from under the stack of papers which constantly littered my desk and read a few pages, searching for anything that would help me through this minefield of emotion. I also prayed for Rich, Lee and the team I had left behind in Iraq.

I had not suddenly become a Christian – in my view a god was just as likely to be a Sikh, Buddhist or Muslim as any other – but for the first time I considered whether more than chance had let me live.

My mind had already shielded me from the most disturbing of my memories and now tried to protect me from further damage. I had taken dozens of photos of the task for evidential and analysis purposes after the task, including photos of the stricken vehicle, crater and forensic evidence. I had shown these photos to a dozen or so people, clicking through them, one after another, safe in the knowledge that there were no upsetting images present. It was as I showed them to Steve Deacon, another ATO who was due to deploy to Iraq, that he stopped me in my tracks:

'Mate.' I looked up from my slideshow and straight at Steve, whose eyes bore into me as he continued.

'You ... you can't see it, can you?'

'See what?' I had seen these photos dozens of times since returning and never noticed anything unusual about any of them.

'That.' His finger rested on the screen. Right in the middle of one of the pictures was one of the casualties. I had never noticed this person; somehow my mind had blocked this out every time I had looked at it. I had subjected unwitting friends to my tour photos and never noticed the look on their faces as that person appeared on screen.

So many of the effects of my trauma were practically invisible to anyone else. No one would know as I sat staring at the newspaper that my mind had disappeared back to Red One and that all I could think of was the smell of death as I walked around the Snatch vehicles. Nor would they guess that as I went to my room in the mess each night I dreaded being alone and could do little to stop the overwhelming anxiety that crushed my chest whenever I thought about Iraq.

Recognizing each symptom was the first step in combating its effect and reducing the damage PTSD could do; I began to develop mechanisms to protect myself from having to re-live the darkest moments of my life. At first they were subconscious, a hundred decisions a day taken to keep me away from the many damaging stimuli that had always been there, but now hurt a lot more. But it was soon clear that I had to make significant, conscious, changes to my life if I was ever going to make progress.

I avoided mess trips to the cinema in Dusseldorf, DVD

nights in the TV room and violent TV in an effort to shield myself from anything that would trigger a relapse. I removed songs from my iPod that would remind me of the task or its immediate aftermath. All but the least horrific photos taken by my team of the scene were deleted in an effort to purge my life of direct links to the day.

And I tried to talk. To anyone.

The range of responses was predictable; from the fascinated to the uninterested; from those who tried to understand, to help and to listen to those who lacked the willingness or ability to care; but even this knowledge did little to soften the blow when friends appeared unwilling or unable to help. I blamed myself. I had obviously misjudged my relationship with those people and thought of us as closer than we actually were.

I had begun to understand that the weight that pressed on my mind was relieved a fraction every time I shared my experience and slowly opened up, wanting to talk more and more. I not only wanted to share the burden of memory but also to look for a cure, a silver bullet that would act as my ticket back to sanity. I wanted a piece of advice, a motto, a shared experience that would help take my pain away.

Most people could not understand what had happened to me. They heard the words as I spoke them, saw the pictures as they appeared on my laptop screen and had even seen footage of the day when it appeared on television, but how could they understand? They had no frame of reference against which to measure the fear and horror of the day, and could not imagine just how terrified we had all been.

This was not their fault, of course; thankfully those people had a narrower range of experience of conflict, violence and trauma and would never understand what it is to give up on your own life.

Whenever I could, often for the most tenuous reason,

I would head back to the Squadron HQ in Bielefeld to see Fitzy. Although we had left theatre a month ago and memories of Al Amarah were not quite as fresh, we managed to talk for hours, often in the squadron bar. While others played drinking games, pool and planned forays into Bielefeld, Fitzy and I grabbed chairs, bottles of Grolsch, and spoke of nothing but Iraq.

Both of us had remained in touch with Jay, and I had frequent emails from Charlie describing the dreadful rocket attacks that rained down on Camp Abu Naji. Fitzy and I clinked our bottles together as we thought of how scared our friends must be. I worried for Jay and hoped that Charlie had managed to add extra energy to the team, to somehow restock Jay's reserves of courage and inspire them to carry on. I was sure he had.

Word of my actions had begun to spread throughout the bomb disposal community. A colonel, who had never served in Iraq, barely knew me and who understood very little about the situation at Red One, called me to say that my judgement had been wrong and that I had put my team into unnecessary danger. That hurt. No one who was with me at Red One had ever questioned my actions. But now, back in the real world, every criticism, however misinformed, tore at my conscience. Had I really risked Jay and Fitzy's life just to prove something to myself?

Meanwhile, it took no more than a note of music, a scene from a film or a moment alone for me to be back there. I felt a mixture of anger, frustration and deep sorrow and felt close to lashing out or breaking down so often it terrified me. I was shattered and could not see any way out of my misery. I had exhausted every avenue in my quest for support, except one.

Beth.

I had spoken to her only once in the last six months and we had exchanged emails at Christmas, but that was it. Nerves gripped me. The last thing she had said to me when we first parted echoed in my head: '*. . . if you ever need me . . .*'

Her phone began ringing. '*. . . I will always be there for you.*' Two rings. Three.

I imagined her looking at the screen on her mobile phone, seeing my name and deciding whether or not to answer.

My heart leapt as I heard her voice.

'Hey dude!' I hated it when she called me dude; this new name seemed to fill the gap between boyfriend and barely friend. Every time she said it I was reminded of the distance between us.

Small talk on her job, my return from Iraq and life in London seemed necessary but was tense. She was doing well: she had a boyfriend, and work was tough, with long hours but interesting enough.

'Beth.' I brought the small talk to an abrupt end. 'Something happened to me in Iraq, something horrible.' I paused to let it sink in. 'I just need to talk.'

'Oh', she sounded scared and intrigued. 'What happened?'

My hand shook as I held the phone, tears welling then racing down my face. I told her what had happened on 28 February, of my conviction that I would die and about the messages I left for her and for my parents.

There was no response. Not a word.

'I just wanted you to know that I was thinking of you.' I sat in my chair, placed the phone on my desk and activated the loudspeaker as I held my head in my hands.

Nothing. I broke the silence.

'Are you OK?'

'Yes, I was just thinking about your silly story.'

It was my turn to be shocked into silence. It didn't last long.

'Beth, I nearly died. I should have died and when I was as close to death as it is possible to be I was thinking of you.'

'You chose it. You chose to put your career ahead of me and now you have to live with the consequences.'

'Would you even care if I had been blown to pieces?'

She said nothing; what could she say?

'OK then.' I searched frantically for words. 'I guess I'll see you around?'

'Yep. See you around.' She ended the call and I sat still, staring at the phone.

She was living her dream and I had lived mine.

16. SEARCHING

March – June 2006

I had been here before: the siren had ripped me violently from sleep but now the rolling barrage of rockets, creeping ever closer to EOD House, pinned me down. My senses were sharp but as the radio crackled constantly, my body was numb:

'Four more inbound from Al Amarah.' My team had heard the same message and now charged around EOD House, their focused activity the absolute opposite of my paralysis. It was only a matter of seconds now, just a few moments before the roof disappeared and took me and the team with it.

The whole earth shook as the first rocket impacted, simultaneously slamming shut the house's thin wooden doors as the blast wave sliced through us. The second and third landed together, the cries from the accommodation tents piercing the thick walls of EOD House and even more terrifying than the deathly shriek of a rocket's terminal velocity.

'WE'VE BEEN FUCKING HIT!' The radio screamed from under my bed.

'We've been fucking hit and have taken casualties.' It was someone in the accommodation; I could hear the chaos behind him as Ops demanded more information:

'Confirm number of casualties, over.'

'I don't know. No one knows – wait out.'

'ATO, this is Ops – confirm location over.'

I should have been heading their way – they needed me now. We were under attack but I couldn't move.

'ATO, this is Ops, over?' I closed my eyes. The casualty report broke the silence:

'Ops, this is the RSM. Confirm that we have two fatalities in the tents. Say again, we have two fatalities and one unexploded bomb. Send ATO, over.'

'ATO, this is Ops – two fatalities and one UXO in the tents – confirm over.'

I still couldn't respond.

The sentry cut in: 'Incoming! This one's gonna hit!'

I hadn't moved since the alarm had sounded. There was one more rocket inbound and this was for me. If only I could get to my body armour and helmet. I reached under the bed.

There was nothing there.

I bolted upright. Within a second, the crisp, cool German air had replaced the smell of burnt clay. The cries, screams and sirens had vanished; in their place, nothing. Silence. I knew I was safe, that there were no rockets, no more casualties and that my war was over, but still my lungs sucked in more air and the sweat poured from my face. It was going to be another long night.

The following evening, less than a month after my return, and only a few days after my conversation with Beth, a group of newly arrived troop commanders returned from a drunken Thursday night in Dusseldorf as I sat in the mess bar, leaning over the day's papers with Paul, a friend who had been in the regiment a year and who was too broke to go out that night.

I had long exhausted my list of excuses for not wanting to venture out and tonight had repeated one of my favourites: I was on duty and could not leave camp in case a call came in.

The peace was broken as Mark, the self-appointed leader of the latest bunch of subalterns, slid along the long seat and put his arm around Paul, who smiled and continued reading his newspaper.

'Where were you tonight, Paul? We fucking missed you!' I glanced up, and then back at the papers.

Mark continued, 'I'm starting to think this mess is full of boring fucking losers – we had a great night in Duss and here you are with your boyfriend reading your stars.' It was stupid drunken nonsense but I looked up again and eyeballed Mark.

'Be quiet, Mark. You're drunk. Don't embarrass yourself.' I spoke slowly, calmly and respectfully but the fire inside had already been lit. The time bomb was ticking down. Mark snorted his disgust but remained silent for a minute before starting to walk towards the bar.

'Fucking losers.' Mark's derision was intended to be loud enough for us to hear but quiet enough for him to deny he had said anything at all.

I exploded.

The small wooden table and its stack of papers flew across the bar floor as pint glasses shattered on the floor in front of me. The bar went silent as Mark turned and saw me charging towards him. Within seconds I was in his face, screaming and pushing my head against his:

'I'm a fucking loser? I'm a fucking loser? Who the fuck are you?' I pushed him back until he thudded against the bar. 'I ought to smash your fucking face in, you fucking prick. Who the fuck are you to walk into this mess and call me anything?' I drew my right hand back to punch but it was grabbed and held by one of Mark's group, who now entered the fray and was dragging us apart.

I had reached rock bottom, willing to punch someone because

he was calling me names. As I watched Mark leave the bar I collected up the papers and pint glasses, replaced the table and as I picked up the fragments of glass, made a decision.

I needed help.

I had felt myself begin to lose control of my emotions since arriving back in camp on 28 February, but my descent had accelerated from the moment Fitzy and I had gone our separate ways upon boarding the plane home.

With only memories of 28 February for company, I had no idea whether I could make it through another weekend. I had worked so hard in Iraq. Others' needs always came before my own. I had needed to overcome crippling fear in order to save others and had only just escaped with my own life. Now I had to find someone to help me.

Anna Smith worked as a civilian doctor at the nearby Joint Headquarters (JHQ) in Rheindalen, but visited our mess every month to hold a clinic in support of our own overworked doctors. In her mid thirties and friendly, I had only met her a few times but knew that, as a doctor, she would be happy to speak to me. I just needed to talk.

The sun baked down on the huge patio that separated the Officers' Mess from its lawn, at the back of which sat a row of tennis courts where friends played cricket, protecting bottles of beer behind coolers and clutching half-eaten hamburgers in their non-bowling hands. It was Friday, work had finished for the week and the mess was in high spirits.

Anna sat on the patio alone, looking towards the lawn as officers roared and a glum-looking captain wandered from the crease clutching his bottle of Grolsch. From the outfield a jubilant signals lieutenant threw a freshly caught tennis ball in the air. I knew it was unfair, that she was off work and needed to relax, but I was desperate. I was already shaking with nerves and had yet to even say hello.

One last deep breath and I walked towards her. My recovery started here.

'A–Anna', nerves made me stutter slightly and I felt sick as she turned and smiled. This was it, the moment I should have taken in Iraq, the time when it is okay to say you have a problem and need help. This was the first step back towards the old me – the real me.

'Anna, I am so sorry to bother you on Friday evening but I think I need help.' She nodded as I continued: 'Something horrible happened to me in Iraq and I can't escape it. I just cannot control my own thoughts anymore.'

She said nothing. Her eyes flicked first towards the cricket and then back to me.

I broke the silence: 'I think I'm losing my mind. I can't sleep. I can't concentrate and every time I close my eyes all I can think about is death.'

Silence once again. Anna smiled at one of the cricketers walking past us to the bar. I looked right at her and begged: 'I need your help.'

It was incredibly difficult to admit to a weakness, but I had done it. I had made the first step. I placed my hands on my forehead as I continued to shake. Relief had washed my nerves away and I fought to avoid the embarrassment of tears.

'OK,' Anna smiled. 'But it's the weekend, and I'm busy next week – so why don't you see how you feel in a couple of weeks?'

I was stunned. 'Weeks?'

'Yep, these things tend to disappear after a few good nights' sleep. Let's see how you feel in a fortnight.'

'But . . .' I stopped myself. Was I being melodramatic? I didn't think so, but Anna's reaction had caused me to wonder. Were my symptoms normal? Had I lost any sense of perspective? A weekend seemed like an impossibly long time. I returned to my room and slumped on to the sofa, my webbing and bergen still in the corner, untouched since I had returned.

I couldn't wait two weeks.

I knew I couldn't wait another day when, a few days later, I saw Rich Holmes sitting on my sofa, watching me silently.

Another doctor, Tim, lived out of camp with his family but visited the mess most nights. My experience with Anna had bruised me. This time I would book an appointment at the med centre, see him on his own turf and ensure that I had his full attention for at least ten minutes. But that night, as I left my block to walk towards the dining room, shivering and slapping my gloved hands together as the bitter German weather bit into my bones, I saw a figure trudging through the puddles toward me. Tim emerged from the gloom and into the light from a lamp that hung off one of the nearby buildings. This is fate, I thought. No one else is around; go for it.

'Hi Tim. How's tricks?' I stopped, avoiding what had now become a steady stream flowing from a burst pipe to the gutter on the opposite side of the road.

'Good mate, thanks.' Everyone is mate in the Army, especially if you don't know each other well.

'Tim, look mate, I need some help. I came back from Iraq recently and am having real problems getting over some of the stuff that happened out there.' There was no way now that I would open my heart to anyone as I had to Anna.

'Can I come and see you and just talk about it? I think I may need to see a shrink.'

'Look, mate – that's quite common. Best just to sit it out for a few weeks, let your mind sort itself out and then decide whether you want help.'

'But Tim – I've started to see some really screwed-up stuff. I'm hallucinating about dead people.'

'You're not the only one who has suffered mate – this is normal. Just hang in there and maybe we can chat when I come back from leave in a couple of weeks.' He saw my eyes close. 'Failing that, go and see Anna.'

I stood as Tim walked past me and into the building I had left only two minutes earlier. Standing in the centre of the road, alone, I realized that this fight was going to be a lot harder than I thought. I wasn't getting it across. It seemed that my inability to communicate with people since Iraq was severely hampering my chances of getting help.

Behind me the stream ebbed by, dragging with it leaves and twigs which were slowly blocking the gutter. Around its edge a small puddle had begun to form. Looking above the door that Tim had just entered I could see rows of icicles hanging dagger-like under the eaves of my accommodation. I took off a glove and scooped a big pile of detritus from the gutter, which gurgled loudly as the puddle shrank. Slowly, more leaves took their place and I walked on.

'Just me and you then, kid' I said to myself.

Third time lucky, I thought, as I pushed open the door of the Bruggen Medical Centre a few weeks after talking to Tim. I had now made an appointment to see another doctor, a different doctor, one I had never met before. So wary was I of rejection that the reason I gave for booking the visit to the receptionist as she took my details was 'back pain'. If I could get a foot in the door, actually see a doctor in their professional environment, there was surely no way they could refuse to help.

Sitting nervously, I leafed through worn copies of *Hello* magazine and looked around me. The smell of disinfectant hung in the air as mothers cradled babies and gently bounced them on their knees.

To the right of reception lay a corridor, off which sprouted the offices occupied by the Combat Medical Technicians (CMTs), Royal Army Medical Corps soldiers who acted as a first line of treatment to soldiers only. Jabs were given, painkillers and biff chits handed out like sweets and tubigrip bandages applied to all but the most horrific injuries.

The other side of reception was calmer, almost serene, and housed the doctors' surgeries. The walls were lined with Jack Vetriano pictures and the floor dotted with tall pot plants which stood guarding the entrance to each surgery.

It was down this corridor that I walked after a man had emerged from his office, dodged a plant and called my name. In his mid forties and wearing the insignia of a lieutenant colonel, he introduced himself as Dr Crew. As we walked toward the office the sounds of soldiers being punctured by CMTs faded into the distance, and the door slammed behind me.

'So, back pain – when do you get it? Dr Crew relaxed into the deep black chair, his hand still half on his computer mouse and his eyes flicking to the screen.

'Actually Sir, my back is fine but, I'm having problems with my mind. I came back from Iraq a month ago and keep having weird thoughts.'

The mouse was moved slowly to one side and Dr Crew dragged his chair directly opposite mine.

'Go on.'

The pressure drained away from me as I explained the events of the day and the problems I was having now.

Time ticked by as I explained in detail every aspect of the operation, of my fears and of the images that would not let go of my conscious mind. The doctor said little, only prompting me occasionally for more detail, to fill in gaps in my explanation and to steer me towards the effects of this trauma. As I spoke, phones were taken off the hook and other appointments ignored. Tears coursed towards my chin as I relived each moment.

When I had finished, the tears had run out and Fitzy and I were safely on the C-130. Dr Crew leant back in his chair.

'You must be crazy ...' My ears pricked up and my heart sank. 'You must be crazy if you think a human can go through everything you have done and not experience side effects.' At last, someone was listening to me. He continued:

'But don't forget, this only happened six weeks ago. That's no time at all for you to recover. I always say to people that if they are still feeling like this after nine months then they should consider seeing a psychologist.'

The elation I had felt initially ebbed away as I exclaimed aloud.

'Nine months!' I couldn't bear the thought of another night alone with my memories, never mind nine months. I sat back in the chair, looked up and exhaled loudly. This wasn't my salvation; this was the beginning of a year of hell. With no help.

I was finished with the Army Medical Services.

My lowest ebb was reached only six months after the event, in August 2006. I had just returned from a holiday in Crete with a friend, where I had spent the last two nights sitting on the beach, staring at the sea and wondering how the hell I was going to escape the curse of this trauma. I was a shadow of the man who had demanded to be allowed to operate in Al Amarah earlier that year in search of war.

I had been left nervous, insecure and could barely control my emotions. As the sun rose and the waves washed against my feet I knew that I was losing my battle. It wasn't just my mind.

I had lost almost two stone in weight and looked increasingly ill.

The day I returned from holiday the news was filled with images of Camp Abu Naji. The camp was handed over to Iraqi authorities on 24 August 2006 and had been ransacked the following day. The Iraqi authorities had been overwhelmed by the locals who had swarmed around the camp and had given up without a fight. The locals had cleared the camp of anything of value: storage units, air-conditioning systems and window frames; they had even stolen the metal sewage pipes.

As it was ransacked, loudspeakers could be heard in the background. Followers of Moqtada Al-Sadr (the leader of the Mahdi army) cheered as the loudspeaker spread the news: 'This is the first Iraqi city that has kicked out the occupiers.'

I sat and watched the camp being torn apart, aflame in areas with thieves stealing truckloads of loot. We had achieved so little: a civil war threatened to break out in Al Amarah and we had just picked up and left.

I was furious. What was the point of being there at all if we were going to leave the town to disintegrate? It seemed that our political masters had neither the willingness to allow the military to do its job properly nor the balls to admit that we had failed. An MOD spokesman said:

'This change reflects the British Forces', growing confidence in the Iraqi Security Forces and their ability to provide routine security in urban areas.'

Twenty-two British lives had been lost in Maysaan province and it tore me apart to think that we would leave without bringing peace to the area, and justice to every single person who had killed a British soldier.

My morale was at rock bottom; my motivation to work was even lower and my self-confidence non-existent. I had started a new job at Headquarters Land, which made me responsible for the development of EOD equipment for the Army, and had rarely felt so distant, so far removed from conflict in Iraq. It seemed from this point on I would be consigned to desk work.

I had no real desire to be a bomb disposal operator again; but the thought of not being able to deploy, never to enjoy that team work and challenge, was too much too bear. This contradiction was at the root of many of my problems. I had become addicted to the adrenalin and action but knew that I had to protect whatever was left of my sanity.

For the first time in my career I also had no clue of what I wanted to do afterwards. Nothing could match the thrill and responsibility of being an IEDD operator. I didn't seem to enjoy desk jobs but I also had to try and protect my mind from the stresses of war.

The clock was ticking; I needed to do something to remove me from the pit of depression and anxiety that had imprisoned me since 28 February.

17. THE LONG WALK BACK

August 2006 onwards

On 6 September 2006 my boss, Colonel Simon Charles and I walked into the office of the Commander-in-Chief of Land Forces, General Watts, ostensibly to brief him on the latest IED threat in Iraq. Colonel Simon and I entered, saluted and the general fired questions at the colonel on the evolution of IED threats in Iraq. What would happen next? How could we counter it? I stood silently, wondering what I could possibly offer to this clash of two intellectual titans. But then the general turned to me.

'And as for you young man, I hear you have been busy in Iraq.' My mouth dropped open as he continued: 'And doing some very brave things indeed.'

My mind went blank.

'And I have the honour of informing you that you have been awarded a gallantry medal for your actions.'

I looked across the room at Colonel Simon, who was smiling back at me. The general continued, 'You have been awarded the George Medal for your bravery. You should be very proud: that award is one level below the Victoria Cross.'

My award, a small circular silver medal with Queen Elizabeth II on the front, an image of St George on the back with a red ribbon with five equally spaced blue stripes, would be received from the Queen at some later date. While incredibly honoured to receive such an award I was much more thankful that the Battle Group, the Brigade, Division and MOD had seen fit to recognize my actions at all. This was the first time since Al Amarah that my decision to risk my team's lives had been publicly backed, and the rush of relief at this vindication over-powered any sense of pride.

I *had* done the right thing.

Since returning from Iraq my actions on 28 February had been questioned by people ranging in rank from private to colonel. Although none of them had been on the ground that day and were not in possession of the full facts, the constant questioning of my judgement began to increase the seeds of doubt in my own mind.

Had I been reckless?

Nights were spent lying awake as I questioned each decision on the day; from the moment I ran to the contact point to conducting the time-consuming isolation or walking to the device without ECM. In the depths of my trauma, I asked myself why my judgement was so bad.

Of course, no one offered any suggestions on how they would have completed the task.

Had I been fatalistic all my life? From my childhood, reading about the Falkland's War and the Troubles had I just been looking for a way to put myself at incredible risk? Had I joined the Army solely to test my own mettle? Did I need to perform some extraordinary action just to prove something to myself or was I just too scared to make the toughest decision of all and say no, it's too dangerous, I can't do it?

A phone call from the blue took me straight back to Red One:

'This is Sergeant Major Tam Russell. Tam! I've just seen a newspaper which says you have been awarded a medal. What did they give you?'

I hadn't heard that voice for six months; I closed my office door, put my feet up and relaxed. Once again I was back in the warm cocoon of comradeship. Tam *knew*. Tam *was there*.

For a single wonderful hour we reminisced about Al Amarah, 28 February and Rich Holmes. There was a movement within the Highlanders Warrant Officers' and Sergeants' Mess to award a trophy annually to the junior officer who could hold his drink least well. Tam had recommended that it be called the Rich Holmes memorial trophy in honour of the hard as nails paratrooper who enjoyed frequent visits to the WOs and Sergeants' Mess nearly as much as he enjoyed soldiering.

'Better than having an annual cross country race in his honour.'

I laughed aloud; Rich would love the idea of poor bastards running miles in his name, but would prefer them to be as drunk as he would be in similar circumstances. Tam had known Rich for far longer than I had, but even in the short time I had known him I understood him well enough to know how he would prefer to be remembered.

Tam and I laughed and were silent in equal measure as we discussed our time in Camp Abu Naji. Even Tam, a hugely experienced man and a giant in the Highlanders, had taken some time to come to terms with that day. If a man like that could take time to get over it, then I definitely could.

As word of my award spread and more stories appeared in the press, I received congratulations from friends, colleagues and, most importantly, the men and women who had shared the experience with me. Amongst the letters I received at that time, one from a general who had known Rich well struck me the hardest. At the end of the typed note he had handwritten a short message:

'Rich Holmes would have been proud of you.' I choked back tears at this simplest of messages.

For the first time since 28 February I began to see the slightest chink of light, a way back from my emotional freefall. I could now begin to look back on my actions through a different lens and see past the idea that I had risked my team unnecessarily.

The award brought no respite from nightmares, aggression or memory loss. But it did provide a glimmer of hope. Maybe there was a path back to normal life; maybe there could be a time when I would escape from thoughts of Red One.

In 2007 I was deployed again to Iraq, this time to Baghdad in a weapons intelligence role, and came across a British platoon who had travelled up from Basra in their Snatch Landrovers. This same platoon had lost two of its men only two weeks earlier: an improvised claymore had detonated as they drove past, sending ball-bearings tearing through the side of the vehicle, which ignited some red phosphorous grenades and killed the two men sitting in the back.

The same platoon were still using the same vehicles and were now tasked with escorting VIPs along Route Irish, between Baghdad Airport and the Green Zone, the most dangerous road in the world.

I stood still, shocked that we were still using these vehicles, and in this of all places. The Americans were replacing every single one of their 13,000 Humvees with huge Mine Resistant Ambush Protected (MRAP) vehicles that were capable of withstanding all but the biggest blasts due to their special armour and blast deflecting V-shaped hulls. Sure, they were expensive, $400,000 each, but countless lives had been saved by the increased protection.

'Don't start, Sir, I know.' The platoon sergeant walked wearily away from his men who sat outside the US PX shop towards me. I looked at him and over his shoulder to the young men laughing outside the shop only metres away. This man and his platoon were chancing their lives every day in vehicles that were inadequate for the job and he knew it.

Nothing had been learnt from the deaths of Rich, Lee and many others in Snatch vehicles; they had little armour to speak of, were too slow and obscured the vision and therefore the situational awareness of everyone inside.

They were not called mobile coffins for no reason; we gave the terrorists the perfect opportunity to kill lots of soldiers with one bomb. They were so used to targeting Snatch vehicles that they had even designed IEDs simultaneously targeting the driver, passengers and top cover. It was like shooting fish in a barrel.

My fists clenched as I turned away from these brave men who had been so woefully equipped, so let down by their political and military masters.

It wasn't just equipment; the bravery of our troops was matched only by the cowardice of the politicians who refused to let us do our job.

We had already given up on Al Amarah, Al Muthana and now, in Basra, British forces had retreated from the city and bunkered down inside Basra Air Station (BAS). We had abandoned the people of Basra and decided that, instead of protecting them, we would cower in BAS, and let the militia take their revenge on anyone who had helped us.

The sergeant told me that inside BAS the soldiers were angry, frustrated and hungry for action. British soldiers always are, but the terriers had been tethered. Armies rot when they are unable to soldier and as the rocketing continued and more lives were lost, morale sank.

It was ultimately left to the US and Iraqi forces to regain control of Basra, and in March 2008 they did. Operation 'Charge of the Knights' swept the militia from the city, improved the quality of life for the citizens of Basra overnight and made more progress in achieving the aim of reconstruction in a few days than the British had made in years.

My disappointment in my political masters compounded my decision to leave the Army, and in June 2008 I handed in my notice. Initially the excitement of a career change dominated my mind; the endless possibilities of starting a new life, a new career and reshaping the person that had been created by an entire adult life in the Army, and most of that as a bomb disposal operator. As the mandatory twelve months notice ticked by, new emotions occupied my mind: guilt, jealousy and confusion conspired to make each thought of leaving the Army family more painful. I was fully aware that I was leaving behind most of what I loved in life and to a large extent what had created my personality.

If I'm not an Army officer, what am I?

My only real achievements in life have been within the Army, principally helping soldiers when they were scared, in danger and no one else had the training to get them out of it. The thought of never being able to help soldiers in such a direct manner ever again tugged at my soul. But I had to leave.

The clerk had no idea of my journey to this point when I handed in my ID card on 4 April 2009. After nearly ten years living my dream, chasing adventure and leading some of the bravest men and women in the world, my last act in the army was to sign my discharge certificate in an anonymous office in Salisbury.

A day earlier I had handed in my uniform and had to choke back tears as my desert combats, the ones I had worn on that day, were thrown in a heap with every other piece of military equipment I had gathered in the last decade. As worthless as these rags were to anyone else they held special memories for me; I had only just managed to save my lucky hat from a similar fate by offering to pay for a replacement.

As I left the gates for the last time I felt sick, with no idea whether I had done the right thing and only certain that I was leaving everything I had loved for my whole working life behind me.

There was no celebration; I was taking the biggest risk of my life in leaving the Army and knew that if it wasn't for my experiences in Iraq I would never have left. In fact I would probably be in Iraq or Afghanistan instead of Wiltshire. When I had resigned nearly a year earlier, I had no job to go to, no grand plan for a radical new career and no other pressures causing me to leave. I just had to go.

My own boss had not even asked me why I was throwing my military career away. If he had asked I could have told him: I wanted more control over my life and needed to protect my mind, not just from the sights and sounds of operations and conflict, but from myself.

The feeling of unfinished business had not left me, some ticking time-bomb inside my own mind which compelled me towards danger every time I was reminded of soldiers in battle. The desire to 'do my bit', which I had first felt in my early teens, had warped into a self-destructive feeling that if I wasn't fighting in some God-forsaken war zone I wasn't really living. Soldiers deserve better than an officer who deploys, not to fight the enemy, but his own demons.

My decision to leave the Army was much tougher, required more thought and was made with much less confidence than my decision to join. My application to Welbeck, the Army Sixth Form College, in 1997, aged just 15, opened endless doors of adventure, excitement and happiness that, nearly twelve years later, I leave behind. The thought of never again experiencing the intimacy that soldiers in combat share, the bond formed by adversity, leaves a hole in my heart far greater than the loss of status, rank or uniform ever could.

But I had one comfort as I walked away from the military. We had lost Rich and Lee and although I was haunted by that, I would also have torn Al Amarah apart to find their killers. I feared that these murderers, like many others in Iraq, would be left free in order to preserve whatever peace there was in Al Amarah.

However, one month after I returned from Al Amarah, an email appeared in my inbox from Will, the Battle Group intelligence officer. As my eyes fell upon the screen I nodded, closed my laptop and sat back in the chair. My friends wouldn't be coming back but justice had been done. For the first time since I had arrived at Red One I smiled. The message was simple.

'Got the fuckers.'

EPILOGUE

Although I didn't realise it at the time, from the moment I looked at Richard lying on the floor, my career was over – and three years after leaving Red One I walked out of barracks for the last time.

But there was really no choice – I had to leave; not only had I used up all of my luck and courage in Al Amarah, but I found I just could not escape the pain of 28 February whilst still being surrounded by graphic reminders of that day. In 2007 I had returned to Iraq to spend four months in Baghdad looking at intelligence reports detailing plots to kill coalition troops; pored over PowerPoint presentations with forensic photographs of dead US and UK soldiers in order to pick up vital clues on bomb technology; spent more time than most climbing through the mangled wreckage of yet more vehicles with the same sickening smell; and every day I mentally revisited Red One and relived every decision, ever ounce of guilt I had felt at surviving.

I was torn between wanting to protect my body and mind, whilst also being driven towards the kind of danger that only combat can provide. I *wanted* to go to Afghanistan; I *wanted* to feel the punch of blast as it passed through my body. I felt worthless because I wasn't on the front line with my mates. Whatever the cause of this irrational lust for action was, it certainly wasn't healthy. A part of me, perhaps a lot of me, felt that I should have died on 28 February and was trying to correct a historical aberration; better men than I had died on the streets of Al Amarah and some very damaged part of my brain felt that I deserved to die too.

I hadn't begun to get over Red One because I hadn't moved on from it; death *was* my life.

Whilst in Baghdad I had attended an EFP incident where all that remained of a US soldier was his body armour and combat helmet. The body armour was covered in blood, leaving only the soldier's velcroed name label visible. The helmet had a small, fifty-pence-coin-sized hole, cut clean through both sides of it; the vehicle smelt like my nightmares. A photograph of the soldier appeared in *Stars and Stripes* a week later. I was just so sick of seeing joy and happiness in the eyes of the dead as they hugged family and friends; so fucking sick, so exhaustingly sick of imagining exactly how each person died. Whereas most people saw a headline on the BBC news and got on with their lives, I read the intelligence reports and dreamed of torn uniform and shredded flesh. I had wanted to spend my career saving lives, but had inadvertently spent more time studying humanity's methods of inflicting the worst kind of suffering on each other. Even when my hands weren't soaked in others' blood, my mind was.

It wasn't just the horror of Al Amarah that had robbed the life from me; I was exhausted. I'd lived more life than people twenty years older than me and was constantly shattered from the constant frenzy of mental activity; my mind spent all day trying to process everything that was harmful, and achieved nothing. It was like there was always something I couldn't quite remember: something at the tip of my tongue, a name or an event or an appointment, and that my mind was constantly trying to recover what was lost. For three years I concentrated non-stop. But it was pointless – I got nowhere. I fantasised of being locked in a dark room for months on end away from noise, images and people. Anything just to give my mind the freedom to do whatever it had to do, to work out whatever it needed to work out, without real life getting in the way and adding even more problems.

By leaving the Army I had finally removed myself from the possibility of seeing war, death or the agony of terror etched on soldiers' faces and, for the first time in my adult life, could look forward to a career without bombs and blood. But I left behind much more than a salary: I left a job I was utterly passionate about – really a job I defined myself by – and the feeling that I could always make a difference. Being in the Army allowed ordinary people to achieve extraordinary things: you could leave school with no qualifications and become an SAS trooper; men and women from underprivileged backgrounds could fly Apache helicopters; we could all become heroes. Bomb disposal wasn't a job; to me it felt like a calling. I hadn't known any other career and, until Red One, had no reason to look.

I was a reluctant civilian, and it hurt.

But, above all else, I knew that the first step out of barracks was my first towards rehabilitation and rediscovering the 'real' me. Or so I thought. I didn't know then, as I threw away a career that had been the focus of my entire adult life, that the toughest mental challenges were still to come.

I'd walked away from an institution where I had, albeit unwittingly, been the beneficiary of an incredible support network. It was OK in the Army to talk about your most damaging memories. Friends had described seeing colleagues, sometimes their best friends, blown to pieces before their eyes. They had tried to convey what it is to enjoy the strongest bonds with someone, a fellow war-fighter, to laugh and to cry and to be silent and to be happy and sad and terrified and then to have nothing; for it to be gone. To lose it all in a thousandth of a second as everything that person knew, stood for and was passionate about was removed from humanity and consigned for ever to fading memories. They too had seen the stillness of death and failed to reconcile those images with the activity and energy of life.

Tough men, battle-hardened soldiers, would drink and cry, stand silently and still as they remembered a friend's last words or last actions. Some would describe how they had to search for the remains of their friends. Men had found themselves collecting the limbs, torso and burnt uniform of a friend who they might have speaking to only minutes earlier. No one else could possibly understand what that felt like; how could they? A person's perception of what was normal was warped so wildly by the memories of hard soldiering that it was difficult to even talk to people who hadn't shared those experiences. In return I'd described seeing Richard and the hopelessness I felt walking towards the bomb. These conversations weren't fun, but they helped, and for many it was as close to treatment as they could get.

My last six weeks as a British Army officer were spent on 'resettlement leave' – an opportunity to retrain for the unknowns of civilian life that lay before me. But I had other plans: my memories of Red One were fading fast – in fact my memory of most things after that day was poor – and getting worse. I felt that no one – friends, family, even if I ever had children – could possibly really understand me, who I was, why I acted in a way different to other people, unless they knew what had happened in Al Amarah. I needed people to read what had happened so they understood why I couldn't watch the news, why I some-times had to excuse myself from family gatherings and just sit on my own or why a red rage developed inside me whenever protestors at troops' homecoming parades shout 'terrorists', 'butchers' or 'murderers'.

So, in February 2009, I started to write it down. Every day for six weeks I sat alone in my spare room and deliberately immersed myself in the feelings of Red One. I listened to Eva Cassidy, Joni Mitchell and the Scots DG band, watched as photographs scrolled along the screen in front of me and wept as solders' home-made videos replayed again and again on YouTube. I thought writing would be cathartic; I thought that by confronting all these emotions during the day I'd somehow escape them at night and be able to move on. I could not have been more wrong. Whilst I enjoyed writing my record of Red One, and for a few weeks felt I was making real progress, I soon found my anxiety levels soaring and my hyper-vigilance made life almost unbearable. I left the Army to escape these stimuli and, as soon as I could, had immersed myself right back in them again.

Without the military support network, and in the alien environment of civilian life, I began to crumble. Symptoms which, until that point, had been slowly creeping into my psyche now began to strangle my mind.

For me, there was no background noise. Every whispered conversation or rustle of a newspaper demanded the same mental focus as a conversation with a friend. My mind was in the middle of a constant tug-of-war between what I wanted to listen to and every other sound that invaded my life and monopolised my conscience. The music from a noisey neighbour would have seemed unreasonable to most people, to me it was agony. I couldn't *not* listen to it. As the bass thump penetrated the walls my rage built up, I felt my chest tighten and I could no longer act like a normal person. I wore earplugs around my flat, remonstrated with the neighbour, moved bedrooms to be further away from the adjoining wall and, on two or three occasions, felt so desperate that I was sure I was going to have a nervous breakdown.

It wasn't just the noise that bothered me; it was that someone didn't care that he was affecting other people's lives. I had, for most of my life, been surrounded by people whom I admired, who had a mutual respect for each other and who often defined themselves by their career. I emerged into the 'real' world and was disgusted. It seemed that society didn't deserve its Army. I, and many others, had willingly risked our lives time and again for our country, some incredible men and women had lost their lives for the same cause. Had the public not seen the pictures of soldiers in combat? Did they not understand that young men and women were performing unimaginably brave acts on their behalf as they complained about last night's television, dropped litter in the street or played their music through the walls of my flat? Everything outside the Army seemed so meaningless. So many people cared only about themselves.

Even away from the stimuli that took me right back to Red One, my mind could not function as it once did. When I trained at the Felix Centre, I had to remember huge amounts of information, discard the less relevant material and produce a robust plan with contingencies for every possible eventuality. I'd spend four to six hours under the most extreme pressure and still be able to operate as well at the end of the day as I had at the beginning. Now it seemed like most of my brain was working on trying to process 28 February, trying to process that *thing*, and whatever remained could barely cope with normal life, never mind a particularly demanding or stressful situation. I reached my mental limit so quickly; colleagues would see my eyes glaze over, and say 'you're there, aren't you?' I would have to pause and let my brain catch up before continuing. It seemed that this illness infected not only my emotions, but my IQ. And my memory was, by now, almost non-existent. I returned home from work each day and couldn't even tell my fiancée what I had done – I just couldn't remember.

Only the chance find of an article in a defence magazine led me to a MoD sponsored scheme for veterans with PTSD.

'It's quite simple.' After a four hour assessment, the psychologist had heard enough. 'Soldiers go through an experience like yours, then they enter multiple relationships, alcohol, drugs and end up on the streets. You've escaped that because you had a rock-solid upbringing.'

So that was it. Forty-three months after Red One I was diagnosed with severe PTSD and mild depression. I was delighted; if he had said – once again – that I should just wait and see, or suggested that this was something a lot of people went through and that I should let it run its course, I would have been devastated; I would just have been a whinger. The PTSD I understood, the depression less so – I didn't always *feel* down.

'Kevin, you have spent the last three hours in this room crying. Of course you are depressed. You have every right to be depressed.'

I was referred, via my GP, to the Maudsley Hospital's Centre for Anxiety and Trauma. There would be a waiting list of four to six months. But just the thought of finally getting a foot on the ladder gave me great hope.

Having just moved house, I clutched my referral letter as I registered with the GP. The initial appointment was with a nurse who, as soon as she closed the door, saw me burst into tears as I handed her the letter. I would be referred as an emergency. But a month passed and I had heard nothing. The receptionist at my GP's was unsympathetic when I called to chase things up: 'Well, if you were referred a month ago and are still with us, it can't be an emergency, can it?'

A further month passed – still no response. I called again. I had seen the wrong person at my initial appointment: a nurse could not refer me. I had to return to see a GP.

'So, you want to be referred to the Maudsley?' I had barely sat down before the GP glanced above the referral letter. 'Do you want drugs?' There had to be more to treatment than this.

A further month passed. Another phone call was made. The GP had faxed the letter but to the wrong number. They would try again. I had been diagnosed two months previously and was, as yet, no closer to treatment than when I had boarded the C-130 from Al Amarah. Two months wasted, and I still wasn't on the waiting list.

In December 2009 I was called forward for an assessment, which would be held a few weeks later. If the Maudsley thought they could treat me, I would finally join the waiting list. Within six months I would finally start to get better.

By the time I reached the Maudsley Hospital, a huge converted town house in Camberwell, London, I had seen six doctors about my condition; the seventh would not have recognised the confident Army Officer who deployed to Iraq four years earlier.

The waiting-room walls were covered with posters discussing obsessive-compulsive disorder and depression. Leaflets offered advice on body dysmorphic disorder and panic disorder. I didn't feel right, certainly didn't feel like I belonged in a place with people suffering from these conditions. It wasn't that long ago I was doing the most difficult job in the world in one of the most dangerous towns in the world. Now I was here. A patient. I had spent a lifetime building up to Red One, but the drop afterward had been at lightning speed.

I had come armed with a handful of questionnaires that had asked me how I felt in social situations; how my traumatic memories felt; whether I considered hurting myself; whether I felt the people viewed me differently because of what I had been through. They were similar to the ones I'd filled in for my initial assessment appointment months earlier, but this time I saw even more of my ticks were towards the right-hand side of the page. Those ticks got a higher score. This was bad.

Two others joined me after a few minutes. One was a woman, perhaps ten years older than me, who carried with her a small bag of shopping and wore the same style of coat as my fiancée. She pulled out a Harry Potter book and began to read. Next in was a young man, perhaps eighteen years old, wearing jeans, a pinstriped suit jacket, white shirt and brown shoes. He, like I, held his iPhone close by and bounced along to barely audible tunes for the few minutes before our psychologists came to collect us.

I wondered what their stories were. I couldn't tell by looking that they belonged here at all. There was no jumpiness, no outbursts. Nothing. They didn't *look* ill. We sat in silence, part of a secret club that no one else would wish to join.

'Kevin, you have severe PTSD, severe depression and the highest possible rating for anxiety.' Shit. It had got worse. Two months of my file bouncing around my GP's office had been incredibly frustrating at the time, but now seemed grossly negligent. While they couldn't send a fax my mind was deteriorating. My psychologist continued: 'But, it's all very treatable, and we can start on Friday if you wish.'

We had barely finished my assessment at the Maudsley when Dr Alicia reached for her diary and opened it at that week's date. 'We can start you on one session a week or, if you wish, try and compress your treatment into a few weeks.'

Silence. She smiled and tilted her head to one side, her eyes widening.

'Is there no waiting list?' Could I really, finally, have made it to treatment?

'Yes – there is. But as a veteran we can prioritise you.'

I'd made it. It was less than a month short of four years from 28 February 2006.

But, to my great surprise, over the next twelve sessions and seven months, I never felt like I received even a moment's therapy. I just talked. To begin with I spoke in detail, excruciating forensic detail, about my tour in Iraq, Red One and its aftermath as Dr Alicia listened and my Dictaphone recorded every word. After each session I had homework: I had to listen to the session and complete another set of questionnaires.

Each session lasted only two or three hours but was utterly exhausting. Dredging through my memory, repeating every single detail and rediscovering old memories was unbelievably hard. Session after session we focused on a narrower chunk of time. After a couple of sessions we had begun to discuss the events of 28 February, then only the time between my 'Contact IED' phone call and the journey back to camp. As I spoke, old memories re-emerged and conversations were brought to life.

What I never expected was that, as I revisited that day, some of my memories would change. The colour of my most shocking memories began to fade from a vivid bright technicolour to sepia. I started to view Richard's body from a different angle. I had remembered standing over his right shoulder before; now I viewed him from his right foot. And it felt right. As these images changed, it felt like it took less and less effort to revisit them, and it was much less painful, too.

Dr Alicia was wonderful; session by session she let me speak, sit in silence and search for words to explain how I felt. We rediscovered memories that had lain untouched for four years, brought them into the open and allowed me to come to terms with them before replacing them. When I listened again to the recordings, I would hear long periods of silence, five or ten minutes of nothing, which, during the session, I had felt, lasted only a few seconds. As I searched for memories I became so engrossed in my own mind that time raced by.

That image of Richard, which for years I had assumed to be burnt into my mind, turned out to be false. I had been so overwhelmed by his death that my mind had tried to piece together the memory as best it could – it was just joining the dots. Now I was rediscovering the memory and, that *thing*, the thing I had to remember, that was always at the tip of my tongue, began to fade away. I was getting my mind back.

As my treatment progressed it became clear that that those few minutes, when I saw Richard, saw the Snatch vehicles, heard and saw the crowd and knew that my own chances of survival were minimal, were just too much for me. I'd been trained to conduct bomb disposal when being shot at; I'd had to operate without Wheelbarrow and ECM before; I'd even been petrol bombed and shot at before. But never all at once. I'd snapped.

There is a part of the brain that controls fear, the bit that, when you step out into the road and see a car coming, drives you back to the kerb. It is designed to sense danger, switch on, get you out of danger and then switch off again. I'd been under threat so often and for such long periods of time that my brain could not switch itself off. Four years after leaving Camp Abu Naji my brain still believed it was at war: I treated everyday sounds like the shriek of a rocket; strangers became an enemy; disagreements escalated to violence. I wore civilian clothes, I was back in real life, I shopped in supermarkets and went to restaurants, but, inside, I was still a soldier; I was still at war.

Further treatment aimed to remove me from the panic I felt whenever unwanted noise entered my life. As I walked towards the bomb at Red One I had no idea that I would find myself sitting beside my therapist on buses as she listened to music, ate apples and talked on her mobile phone – anything to help me use public transport without seething with anger at my fellow passengers.

My treatment ended in August 2010. Within two months of starting it I had felt like a completely different person and by the end I was – almost – the 'old' me again. The symptoms of

PTSD may be on the wane, but I cannot expect to go through something like Red One and be exactly the same as I was before – and I wouldn't want to either. Leaving Dr Alicia felt a lot like riding a bike without stabilisers for the first time; every now and then I wobble, but I've yet to crash, and I cannot see that happening in the future either.

I'm delighted, of course, that the treatment had such a positive effect; but it makes my blood boil to know that, over four years earlier, I *knew* I needed help, I *knew* the right course of treatment would save me from the worst of PTSD, and yet I couldn't get it. And if I, a middle-class, well-educated Army Officer with every advantage in the world, couldn't get help, spare a thought for the soldiers without all those advantages.

However, the MoD is certainly doing more than before: a formal system for the identification of vulnerable soldiers has empowered the chain of command to assist soldiers who have been exposed to the most disturbing events; operational theatres are visited by psychiatrists more frequently and troops formally 'decompress' (a period to mentally unwind between an operational deployment and home) before being dropped into family life.

But much more is required. The Surgeon General, Lieutenant General Louis Lillywhite, said in 2009: '*Only four per cent of those that deploy will suffer from PTSD ... we do not have a time bomb waiting to go off... PTSD is [not] a major concern.*' Until we appreciate the scale of this problem, we cannot possibly hope to correctly resource its treatment; the MoD's own figures suggest that 7 per cent of *combat* troops suffer from PTSD and that, in specific at-risk groups, the figure may be much higher. But this isn't just an MoD issue. I was treated by the NHS, and if we want soldiers who, like those in the British Army, are willing to undertake the most horrific actions imaginable for the benefit of our country, we are obliged to use all the resources of defence, wider government and society to look after them when they come home.

So, we are making progress. But we're not there yet. In September 2010 a fellow bomb disposal operator told me that he had recently been referred to a non-MoD PTSD specialist; mentally, he too had yet to leave Iraq and could not escape the memories that had been seared into his mind. He had poured his heart out, opened his soul and taken the first steps towards his recovery.

The advice? Give it nine months and see how you feel.

For four years I tried to get the treatment I knew I needed from the moment I saw Richard Holmes lying on the Red Route. I've had some pretty low moments, wondered whether my brain would be able to cope with life and whether I'd ever recover the old me again. There were many times when I came close to giving up, and some when I thought I had beaten it only to be dragged back into its clutches again.

But I really did have it easy. We have lost five of our best ATOs in the past two years, with many more wounded. I knew each one: I had known Dan Shepherd since we were 16, had shared illicit beers with Gary O'Donnell in Northern Ireland and had enormous respect for Dan Read, Oz Schmid and Brett Linley. Even the most skilful operators can only roll the dice so many times. The Royal Engineer Search Teams – so crucial in detecting IEDs – have lost even more and, as has always been the case, the infantry and other combat arms have taken the brunt of the losses. What I did in Iraq was tough, demanding soldiering; what our troops are doing each day in Afghanistan is many times harder. I've heard of soldiers who are under so much threat that they are sick through fear when they leave camp. But leave camp they do, that day, and the one after, and the one after; they don't let their mates down, and I am in awe of every single one of them.

Closer to home, my PTSD was tough, but many others have faced far greater challenges. In July 2009 Private Andrew Watson threw himself to his death after watching television coverage of the repatriation of eight soldiers who had died in Afghanistan. His family said he was tormented by his Iraq experience, during which he saw two of his friends blown up by a mine and carried the bodies of dead babies out of buildings. We ask our soldiers to do unbelievable, horrific things on our behalf, and they will do it for us, but we owe them every support possible when they return.

My PTSD was only severe; some are critical – I dread to think how that feels.

I have the most amazing family a man could wish for. My parents have always put their children first. My father inspires me with his honesty and decency and my mother's selflessness is extraordinary – when I wanted to go to Welbeck, the Army boarding school, she took a second job, at a fast-food restaurant in the evenings and at weekends, in order to pay the bills. My sister leads the most incredible life and has two wonderful children of her own. My wife and son mean the world to me, and I am incredibly blessed to have been surrounded by the most caring people you can imagine when I have been at my lowest.

I met a lot of amazing people in the Army: some were brilliant strategists, some were inspirational leaders, some were even heroes. But not one of them was a superman. A number have walked down the same path as me; we are ordinary people, reacting in a very ordinary way, to some extraordinary events.

Every time I see soldiers these days I try and take a moment to wonder what their personal story might be. Whether they are marching in front of the Queen or fighting in Afghanistan, there's a damn good chance that they will have achieved feats beyond the comprehension of most. Many will have lost mates in combat, some will have been soaked in the blood of friends as they spoke their last words and all of them will never forget the sights, smells and sounds of combat. Under that bearskin lies a warrior; beneath the peaked cap sits a hero; the camouflage paint can protect a man from the enemy, but it cannot hide the sadness in eyes that have seen too much; nor can the move from soldier to civilian.

I am on the road to recovery and sometimes even reminisce about Iraq, Al Amarah and its citizens, most of whom just wanted to live in peace. Thinking of Red One, I see the long straight road sweeping from west to east, the Olympic stadium looming to the south and the tall flats from which people watched the world pass by each day. Young children with huge smiles run toward soldiers asking for water, sweets and dollars and older brothers sell trinkets, posters and DVDs to British troops patrolling the ground, each stopping to talk to any local who wished.

In the centre of all of this I see Rich and Lee, dressed in full combat dress, faces covered with the dust swirling around them, their Parachute Regiment insignia on show for all to see. Laden with weaponry, webbing, grenades and wearing their Para helmets and with the huge smiles that they so often wore when soldiering, they look every bit the toughest soldiers in the world. I don't like to imagine them any other way.

As for my mind? It's been a tough road so far, and there is a long journey ahead. But I'm a better person for it.

ACRONYMS

1 QLR	1st Battalion, The Queen's Lancashire Regiment
2IC	Second in Command
Al Mak	Local name for Al Majar Al Kabir
APC	Armoured Personnel Carrier
ARF	Airborne Reaction Force
ASM	Artificer Sergeant Major
ATO	Ammunition Technical Officer 'Felix'
BAOR	British Army of the Rhine
BAS	Basra Air Station
CIMIC	Civil-Military Co-operation
CO	Commanding Officer
ECM	Electronic Countermeasures
EFP	Explosively Formed Projectile
EOD	Explosive Ordnance Disposal
FFD	First Field Dressing
GPMG	General Purpose Machine-Gun
HLS	Helicopter Landing Site
ICP	Incident Control Point
IED	Improvised Explosive Device
IEDD	Improvised Explosive Device Disposal
IRA	Irish Republican Army
IRGC	Iranian Revolutionary Guard Corps
ISAF	International Security and Assistance Force
JDAM	Joint Direct Attack Munition
PJHQ	Permanent Joint Headquarters

LECs	Locally Employed Civilians
Minimi	A belt-fed light machine gun
MOD	Ministry of Defence
MRAP	Mine Resistant Ambush Protected vehicles
MSR	Main Supply Route
NCO	Non-Commissioned Officer
OC	Officer Commanding
PIR	Passive Infra Red detector/switch
PIRA	Provisional IRA
PJOC	Police Joint Operations Centre
PRR	Personal Role Radio
PSNI	Police Service of Northern Ireland
PTSD	Post Traumatic Stress Disorder
PWRR	Princess of Wales Royal Regiment
QRF	Quick Reaction Force
REME	Royal Electrical and Mechanical Engineers
RESA	Royal Engineers Search Advisor
REST	Royal Engineer Search Team
RMCS	Royal Military College of Science, Shrivenham or 'Shriv'
RPG	Rocket-Propelled Grenade
RSM	Regimental Sergeant Major
SAM	Surface to Air Missile
SAT	Senior Ammunition Technician
SBS	Special Boat Service
SUSAT	Sight Unit Small Arms, Trilux sights of men's SA8os
TACP	Tactical Air Control Party
WIS	Weapons Intelligence Section
WO1	Warrant Officer (Class One)